THE ORIGINAL
ROCKET
RECALL
TEACH YOUR DOG TO COME

Lisa Lyle Waggoner
CPDT-KA, CSAT, PMCT2

Cold Nose College Publishing
Murphy, North Carolina

The Original Rocket Recall, Teach Your Dog to Come/Lisa Lyle Waggoner.
—1st ed.

Published by:
Cold Nose College Publishing,
a division of Cold Nose College, LLC
Murphy, NC 28906
www.coldnosecollege.com

Cover design by:
Deana Stranz
Stranz Creative

Photo Credits:
Hannah Lozano, Hannah Lozano Photography
Bonita Ash, Ashford Studio
Lisa Waggoner

Illustration Credits:
Denise O'Moore, Mighty Dog Graphics

The Original Rocket Recall: Teach Your Dog to Come
ISBN: 979-8-9856580-0-2

Library of Congress Control Number: 2022933408

In Praise of
The Original Rocket Recall: Teach Your Dog to Come:

"Whether you're a pro trainer, a dedicated training hobbyist, or a brand new dog lover, Lisa's *Rocket Recall* is the definitive guide for teaching a fast, reliable recall—and having fun doing it."
— **Veronica Boutelle, MA Ed., CTC, Founder of dog*biz**

"A reliable recall is one of the greatest gifts you can give your beloved canine companion, allowing him to stay safe while having much greater freedom and many more opportunities to explore his world without the annoying, constant constraint of a leash. Lisa Waggoner's *Rocket Recall* is an incredibly valuable gift to the dog-loving world, sharing sound, scientific, and effective positive reinforcement-based methods that can only strengthen relationships between dogs and their humans, and enhance the quality of life for both. Lisa is a superb teacher and trainer and an excellent writer. This book deserves to be read and put into practice by everyone who wants to give their dogs the best life possible."
— **Pat Miller, CBCC-KA, CPDT-KA, Author of 7 books on dog training and behavior, including *The Power of Positive Dog Training*, and *Beware of the Dog***

"*Rocket Recall* is a must-have guide for every training library. Lisa Lyle Waggoner has created a training process that makes your dog want to come in any environment. By focusing on positive reinforcement, Waggoner has developed techniques that create effective and lasting communication with our dogs. It is filled with easy-to-follow lessons that not only make life with dogs easier, but may save their life."

—Dr. Lynn Stevenson, MA, DVM, Nottely Oaks Animal Hospital

"Sure, it's a thrill to see my dog turn and race toward me when I call, but the deeper value of Rocket Recall was to create a bond of trust and affection with my dog. Lisa Waggoner's clear, methodical instructions guaranteed training was fun for both us and assured us of success. Rocket Recall taught me how to become my dog's best friend."

—Sharon Coogle, Dog Devotee and Cold Nose College Graduate

"*Rocket Recall* is a complete training manual that every dog owner and professional trainer should memorize. My favorite parts were when Waggoner talks about her own dogs and the challenges she encountered and then overcame. The training games are fun, and the Quick Reference Guide is a winner—for the non-professional trainer or new dog owner it will be invaluable."

— Eva Shaw, PhD, Author of *The Seer*

"Lisa Lyle Waggoner's new book is a must-have for all dog lovers. She balances a narrative between the touching story of her own journey learned alongside family canine companions to lightbulb moments that led her to become a certified professional trainer. Lisa advocates for behavior science and its value in crafting training plans. Her inclusion and citations of colleague tips along with her own showcase what a collaboration should be—us learning joyfully together with our dogs. Lisa's practical tips for rocket recalls support relatable examples that also support and empathize with the normal frustrations and expectations of dog owners. Want to learn more about how the Three Ds, the value of antecedents and consequences, distraction hierarchy, reinforcement value, suggested equipment for the dog team, wildlife safety, and meeting the dog and handlers needs where they are with their fluency skills? Then this excellent resource is for you. Her breakdown of phases in each exercise offers insight into what TO DO when training doesn't go as planned. My dogs love the "Hide and Go Seek" and "Recall and Release" games! Lisa's "12 Rules of a Rocket Recall" should have one more rule; run to add this amazing book to your library!"

— **Laura Monaco Torelli, KPA CTP, CPDT-KA**

For Abbey.

If only I had known then what I know now.

Contents

Acknowledgements

MY BOUNDLESS GRATITUDE goes to my cherished dogs, past and present: Abbey, Carter, Gibson, Cody, Willow, and Cailie. Each one taught me more about life and dog training than I ever expected to learn.

I offer a heartfelt thanks to every client I've had the privilege to work with over the years. Thanks for embracing my training techniques. Your questions, comments, and success with your dogs encouraged and motivated me to create and hone the recall training methodology in this book. You inspire me, always.

Every writer should be graced with unwavering support from a talented editor. Eileen Anderson is that and much more. Her keen eye for detail of the written word and her understanding of dog training have been invaluable in bringing this book to fruition. I'm ever grateful our paths crossed. Should you find an error, point a finger at me—I continued to tweak the content long after receiving Eileen's edits.

Steve White, Eva Shaw, Sharon Coogle, Pat Miller, Veronica Boutelle, Laura Monaco Torelli, and Dr. Lynn Stevenson, who were kind enough to give their time to read an advance copy of this book, have my sincere thanks. Your comments and suggestions enhanced my work.

Thanks also to Denise O'Moore of Mighty Dog Graphics for her fantastic illustrations. I feel more than lucky to find such talent in a person who also happens to be a professional dog trainer. And to the professional photographers Bonita Ash and Hannah Lozano, thank you for your keen eye in helping me portray the training techniques described in this book. A big shout of thanks also goes to Hannah's husband, Anthony, and their adorable dog, Mia, for agreeing to be subjects in many of the photos you see in the training sections of the book.

What would a book be without a beautiful cover? Deana Stranz of Stranz Creative has been doing graphic design for Cold Nose College for nearly two decades. She never disappoints and is always a joy to work with—thank you, Deana, for your amazing talent. And speaking of the cover, thanks to our dear friends Walter and TonI Bahn. Your perspectives about the draft cover design helped bring about the perfect book cover.

I'm grateful to Tyler Barber for his experience and skill with interior book design and for knowing how to best present my text and the many photos and illustrations portraying the training techniques. A big thank you also goes to John Rose of Glass Bead Editorial for his skill in indexing the contents. And kudos to Mychelle Garrigan of Pet Pro Marketing and Firelink Digital for her help with all things website, including the book's promotional page on the Cold Nose College website.

And last, but definitely not least, thank you to Brad, my partner in life and business. Without him this book wouldn't have been possible. No matter the time of day or night when an idea or a question about the content in this book would pop into my brain, he'd kindly listen and share his always objective and sound feedback. Thank you with all my heart.

Foreword

THROUGH THE YEARS, I had seen Lisa Lyle Waggoner at professional dog training conferences before but didn't really know her. This time we happened to be in the same hotel in Asheville, North Carolina, where I was going to teach a weekend workshop. She had an adorable little pup named Willow that reminded me so much of my old drug dog, Spud, that I just had to stare as she loaded her into her van outside the hotel.

Once my shock at the similarity wore off, I was transfixed watching the clarity and mindfulness of Lisa's interactions with Willow. I'm a sucker for watching anybody who is good at what they do. It was immediately apparent that Lisa had put in the work to build exceptional skills. Later, I was delighted to see that Lisa and Willow attended the workshop. They did not disappoint. Even at such a tender age, Willow stole the show, trusting Lisa would never ask her for a behavior she couldn't perform. Lisa never broke that trust and exquisitely reinforced Willow's progress.

As you read *The Original Rocket Recall*, you're in for a similar treat. Lisa is every bit as good at conveying how to train as she is at the training itself. Her training and writing styles are elegant. There is no wasted effort. Everything has a purpose, fits into the plan, and is broken down into easily digested chunks. Foundations are laid before adding intricacies. Skills are incrementally built to address the unexpected. When you run into one of those inevitable bumps in the road, it's easy to back up to a point of success and build even stronger behaviors from there. The finished product of such training is a dog that, despite distractions, comes right away when called.

The finished product of this book is a roadmap for you to do the same...if you follow Lisa's clear plan. I'm not kidding. For years I used videos of Lisa's dogs' recalls to inspire police K9 handlers to improve their dogs' recalls. Lisa provides just the right amount of science to explain why the method works so well. Even better, the exercises are fun for both you and your dog. As you follow the Rocket Recall plan, you'll also build a dog that remains attentive when with you. With recalls and attention established, the sky's the limit as to what you two can do together.

I recommend you read this book from start to finish before wading into the training. Once you understand both the plan and underlying principles, you can more effectively map out your training. From there, it's just a matter of having fun as you set up your dog (and yourself) for success after success. If you do this, the process will be so enjoyable for you both that it will become a lifestyle. Life with dogs doesn't get much better than that.

- **Steve White**, *working dog consultant and retired police K9 trainer/ supervisor*

[1]

Introduction

BRINGING THIS BOOK into the world has been a desire of mine for a very long time. In 2015 at an outdoor social for our clients and their off-leash dogs, my girl, Willow, joined in the fun. In addition to helping her continue to enjoy the company of a variety of other dogs, I also used the outdoor socials to practice recall. Over the course of 45 minutes, I called her to me six or eight times and each recall was met with this success: Willow leaving the action and returning to me immediately, enthusiastically, and with rocket-like speed. One client asked, "How in the world do you do that?" My simple answer was, "You train it."

Not long after the outdoor social I wrote an article for Whole Dog Journal about my recall training methodology, then my husband and business partner, Brad Waggoner, and I filmed a rocket recall how-to DVD with Tawzer Dog. The DVD is now available via streaming. This book was next on my to-do list, but the responsibilities of a busy dog trainer and life in general placed my focus elsewhere.

Willow departed this world very unexpectedly at only six years of age. To say that my world turned black and white is an understatement. I wasn't sure how to move forward in life without her or even if I could. I had soared knowing I was her person. Without her beside me I was lost. When her heart stopped beating, I felt as if mine had stopped, too. Willow changed my life in immeasurable ways—and the lives of others from her work as a canine teacher in our business. We were inseparable. The extraordinary bond we shared was visible to anyone who saw us together.

Beyond my boundless love for Willow, the results of her training were a shining example of how my training skills had grown over the years, including the way I blended a variety of training exercises to achieve a solid recall, known as the call to come. When she died, I lost the impetus to do most anything, including writing this book.

I put a lot of training hours into honing Willow's recall skills and every single moment of training was joyful for both of us. That's the thing about positive reinforcement training. You gain immediate buy-in from your dog resulting in unbridled enthusiasm. No doubt my skills and our solid partnership brought about success, yet somewhere in the recesses of my mind, I thought I was merely lucky to have a dog who learned so easily. No matter that I had trained Willow's predecessor, Gibson, in the same way with the same success. I still thought I'd been lucky.

Enter Cailie, my now three-year-old, red tricolor Australian Shepherd. She joined our home only a month after Willow left us. Too soon in some respects, though in other ways she saved me from me. I was overtaken with grief and putting all my focus on training my over-the-top adorable, vibrant, spunky puppy was a wonderful coping mechanism.

I applied the same recall training techniques with Cailie that I did with Gibson and Willow. Seemingly before I could blink when I called her from the back of our pasture with her recall cue, "Ca-Ca-Come" ("Ca-Ca" delivered in a staccato-like sound and "Come" more drawn out—"Coooooome") she'd turn on a dime and with blazing speed skid into my feet like a baseball player sliding into home plate. It thrilled me. Yet again I achieved a Rocket Recall.

I believe you can, too—and without resorting to aversive training techniques that may include choke collars, pinch collars, or heaven forbid, a shock collar. There are a variety of studies with results showing the benefits of positive reinforcement, many of which you'll find on companionanimalpsychology.com, the website of Zazie Todd, PhD. I want my dog to feel physically safe, emotionally safe, and joyful during the learning process.

As you move through the text within these pages, you'll notice grammar choices I made when referring to a dog or multiple dogs, in particular gender. I pondered all the usages. Brad and I have both a male and female dog in our home, so that was of no help to me in deciding. I certainly wasn't going to use "it"—often recommended—using "it" for a sentient being was out of the question for me. In the end, I decided to use the male pronoun "he" when referring to a dog and the female pronoun "she" when referring to the trainer, and I use the plural "they" or "them" when appropriate. I trust this doesn't offend you. As you read this book, feel free to insert your gender and your own dog's gender as you read.

The Rocket Recall training methodology in this book has been tried and tested with incredible results by hundreds of our clients. All you need is a willing attitude and a desire to learn. Oh, and a dog!

[2]

How I Developed My Training Philosophy

HERE I AM a professional dog trainer. If twenty years ago someone had said, "Lisa, you'll be a dog trainer," I would have chuckled and said, "Ah, get outta here. You're crazy."

I want you to understand my training philosophy—what it was, how and why it changed, and where it is today.

It was the tragic death of a dog that propelled me on the path toward dog training. My husband, Brad (also now a professional dog trainer), and I rescued a stray, mixed-breed dog in 1996 whom we named Abbey. Living in Marietta, Georgia, a suburb of Atlanta, we wanted her to be a well-trained dog, so we called around in search of a local dog trainer until we found a training class near our home.

On the first night of class, we were issued a leather leash, a choke collar, a prong collar, a six-inch tether, and a fleece mat. We were taught how to jerk on the leash to correct Abbey when she did something we didn't like. We learned how to step on the leash quickly, and with force, to make her lie down. With one end of the tether attached to the baseboard and the other end attached to her choke chain around her neck, we learned to walk away from her and only return when she gave up struggling. We learned how to alpha roll her when she snapped at another dog to purportedly show her we were the boss.

We were told to practice what we learned in class in different places, so I took Abbey to a nearby strip mall shopping center to practice loose leash walking on the sidewalk. It was during this trip I first felt what I was doing to my dog was wrong.

Abbey was dressed in her usual training gear: a choke collar and a prong collar (also known as a pinch collar). The leash was attached to the prong collar. As instructed, I gave the "heel" command and started walking at a brisk pace. Abbey followed. Then also as instructed and without any forewarning to Abbey, I did an about-face. But Abbey kept walking forward, so I yanked hard on the leash while turning around to look at her. What I saw on her face was confusion and fear. Fear of me.

I didn't understand dog body language back then, but I knew enough to understand that Abbey didn't enjoy what I did to her and certainly didn't understand why I did it. I think she wondered why I hurt her. Oh yes, she did hurry to catch up with me and I praised her as she did, though she had a sad look in her eyes. Not the happy face I had seen when we got out of the car. We didn't know enough to question the training techniques we were taught. We continued in class, learned well, and Abbey graduated with honors.

In December of 2000, we added a blue merle Australian Shepherd, Carter, to our home. By then we'd moved from the city to our country home here in Murphy, North Carolina. After attending a short puppy kindergarten class locally we wanted to carry on with further training.

We decided Carter should follow in the paw steps of Abbey and attend the Marietta dog training class. It had been four years since Abbey graduated. We felt she could use a refresher and enrolled both dogs. Crazy to think we drove four hours round trip each Monday to the same facility where we took with Abbey in 1996. Carter was bouncy and happy in class, but Abbey was different this time—she didn't want to get out of the car. We managed to coax her out of the vehicle and into class, but it was becoming evident to us she didn't enjoy anything inside or outside that building.

Now that I had an Australian Shepherd, I set my sights on agility. A few people I knew who had Aussies were doing agility. It looked like such fun! There were no classes near me, so I bought a couple of agility training books. The training techniques in each of the books were different from what I learned in our dog training class.

Each book suggested using food to reinforce the dog when he made even the slightest bit of progress with an agility obstacle. This was all new to me and I liked it. I started using food. Carter's exuberance and the effectiveness of this new way of training amazed me.

I saw nothing but joy and excitement in Carter's eyes versus the uncertainty and fear I'd seen in Abbey's eyes when I was using the choke and prong collars. I thought, "Wow, I don't have to hurt my dog to train my dog? I have immediate buy-in—he's such a willing partner!"

I had just discovered positive reinforcement training. Carter was my crossover dog, though I didn't know the term at the time. I had crossed over from using aversive training to positive reinforcement training.

We continued to have all sorts of success with the backyard agility equipment I purchased. On Wednesday, March 13, 2003, we took our first competition agility lesson in Woodstock, Georgia. You should have seen Carter's confidence while negotiating the new, never-before-seen obstacles. I was one proud Dog Mom. Little did I know that was the last time we would ever enjoy agility together.

Three days later, the morning of Saturday, March 15, Carter was hit by a car, his back broken in two places and his spinal cord severed. Euthanasia was the only option. It took me three months to climb out of what I now know was depression. I emerged thinking, "I want to help others learn there's a different way to train their dog."

I was eager to use my newfound training methodology on another dog. Gibson, a handsome, blue merle Australian Shepherd puppy, joined our home in June of 2003, only a few months after Carter left us. With him by my side, I honed my positive reinforcement dog training skills and again achieved successful results. He left us at only eight years of age as a result of hemangioscarcoma.

When Abbey passed away in 2008 after living a long, happy life, we adopted Cody, a two-year-old, red merle Australian Shepherd. Brad was Cody's trainer and honed his own positive training skills with our new, fractious boy. How joyful it was to bounce training ideas off one another to overcome common training challenges. In February of 2012, Willow joined our home and my positive reinforcement training journey continued.

So here I am many years later, a professionally educated, certified professional dog trainer who uses positive reinforcement to train dogs. I believe in humane training. No dog should suffer physical pain or even mild discomfort during training. If a dog feels pain or discomfort during training, learning is difficult, if not impossible. Dogs are living, breathing, sentient beings with needs and wants. I want to meet every single one of my dogs' needs and most of their wants.

And I advocate for my dogs. To me, advocating for my dogs means putting the physical and emotional well-being of my dogs before my own needs. This includes protecting my dogs from injury, from other dogs, and from other people. It also means I may need to speak up for my dogs in a variety of situations because they don't have the ability to do so. Being my dog's advocate builds trust between us. I want my dog to trust that I will put her only into situations that she can comfortably handle.

Trust. It's an important component in a relationship. It's also an important component in a teacher and learner relationship. The information and training exercises in this book are designed to not only help you learn how to teach your dog to come, but also build trust along the way.

With trust, the seemingly impossible becomes possible.

[3]

What Is a Rocket Recall?

I DEFINE A ROCKET RECALL as "That glorious moment when anytime and anywhere you say "Come!" and your dog immediately and enthusiastically turns on a dime and bounds rapidly to you." Sound impossible? It's not. It *can* be done.

The recall training protocol is designed for a dog who is already comfortable in your home. The dog should be affiliative with people and other dogs outside of your social circle and in new locations. If your dog displays any fear, reactivity, or aggression to people or other dogs, those behavioral challenges should be addressed first before launching into Rocket Recall training.

I tell clients an indoor, off-leash recall is like a high school diploma—pretty easy to get—but an off-leash, outdoor recall is like a PhD. Admittedly, that's quite an exaggeration, but it gets the point across. A reliable Rocket Recall just doesn't miraculously happen.

The goal of the training exercises in this book is to help you teach your dog a successful recall in both known and new locations. Your dog will master the skills in a known location and your recall will be reliable in that one area, but you must continue training to help your dog learn to return to you in a new location. A new location is ever so much more distracting. The squirrels, the new pee smells!

You'll gain the skills to train through distractions to success. There will always be a myriad of new visual and olfactory distractions in brand new locations that will inevitably cause your dog to give you "that look" when you call as if to say, "Surely, you don't mean now...with all this wonderful stuff for me to explore?"

You're going to learn the systematic way of training recall that we've used with hundreds of dogs and clients at Cold Nose College for over a decade, how to problem-solve speed bumps you encounter along the way, common training mistakes, considerations for training around prey, and we'll wind up with the 12 Rules of Rocket Recall, a list of very important things to remember during your journey.

Understanding the definition of systematic is important. Merriam-Webster defines systematic this way:

"methodical in procedure or plan" (Merriam-Webster, n.d.).

I want you to be methodical in planning recall training for your dog. The training exercises in this book are designed to be understood, practiced, and applied using the four stages of learning I describe later in the book. Once you achieve consistent success with each individual exercise, you'll learn how to combine the exercises to bring about further success.

Now let me add a caveat. Your dog has a genetic predisposition to alert, orient toward, and chase prey animals (and yes, sometimes kill and eat them). Some dogs have a higher propensity than others to find, chase, and capture prey. There is always a chance your dog could choose prey over your Rocket Recall cue. I strongly advise you to always practice recall in a safe, enclosed space. Early in my career, I took risks with Gibson and Willow that I would never take today with Cailie. My dog is precious to me and risking her death for an off-leash romp in an unknown, unenclosed space is a risk I no longer wish to consider. There's such a thing as deadly trust. I will always err on the side of safety for my dog's well-being.

[4]

Understanding How Dogs Learn

I ADMIT IT. I can geek out talking and thinking about learning theory. There are many different ways of defining learning theory, some of which make even my eyes glaze over. Think of learning theory as a framework that describes how a dog or person absorbs, processes, and retains knowledge during learning.

I love dogs and people and because I'm a professional dog trainer, understanding learning theory helps me problem solve dog training issues, find effective ways to help my human clients learn, and helps me ensure my learners (dogs and people) feel safe and happy during the learning process. I want both the dog and the client I work with to retain the knowledge I impart during a training session. That's what I want for you, too.

Having some degree of knowledge about how dogs learn will aid you in training your dog, not just for recall, but for anything else you want your dog to learn. You'll be able to understand why the training exercises in this book work. When something doesn't go just right in a training session, you'll be able to problem solve the issue to bring about success. Learning never happens in a straight line, so problem-solving skills are always necessary.

When's the last time you learned something new? Maybe it was learning a new musical instrument or learning to knit. Whatever the skill, I suspect you felt a bit of stress (or even frustration) trying to tackle the new skill. It's that way for our dogs too.

The goal is to help a dog feel as comfortable as possible while teaching him a new skill. The same goes for you. You'll be learning new skills, so please be easy on yourself when absorbing the new material. The most effective learning takes place when both you and your dog are comfortable and happy.

"So how do dogs learn?" you ask.

Dogs learn by association (what's safe and what's not) and by consequence (is this good for me or bad for me?). Learning by association is known as Classical Conditioning and learning by consequence is known as Operant Conditioning.

Stick with me through this section—understanding how your actions and training choices affect your dog will help guide you through to successful results.

Feel free to refer to the glossary at the back of the book for further reference when you encounter a technical term.

Classical Conditioning

Does the name Pavlov ring a bell? Some of you may be familiar with the work of Ivan Pavlov. He's the scientist who helped us understand classical conditioning. In fact, many learning theorists still refer to classical conditioning as Pavlovian Conditioning.

"Classical conditioning refers to the process by which an animal learns to associate events over which it has no control. Classical conditioning is the type of learning in which the conditioned stimulus (such as the sound of a bell) is paired with and precedes the unconditioned stimulus (such as the sight of food) until the conditioned stimulus alone is sufficient to elicit the response (such as the salivation of a dog). This learning enables the animal to predict the occurrence of events in its environment and adapt to them before they happen." (McGreevy and Boakes, 2007, 31).

What's important to remember about classical conditioning is that your dog is making an association every moment in response to a particular stimulus. That association could be positive (happy) or negative (unhappy) or even neutral (just so-so). Because of the "association," the dog may really enjoy a certain location (the park where fun walks are taken) or a piece of equipment (the leash, which means a walk) or the dog could be fearful or afraid of the stimulus (the person, place, or thing), based on the prior "association" with that stimulus. Remember, the dog doesn't have to think about the association—the dog has an emotional response to a particular stimulus. Dogs are making decisions every moment about their environment.

Here are two examples of learning by association:

Human example:
As I child I lived in Oklahoma and our house was situated at the edge of a wheat field abundant with tarantulas. My mother was terrified of those big, hairy creatures. Each time one appeared

Because of repeated exposures to my mother's fearful behavior and resultant actions, it took only one or two more times of seeing a tarantula (anywhere around our home) for me to become afraid not just of tarantulas, but of all large brown spiders.

in the house or on the front porch she'd scream, grab my arm, and steer me as far away as possible from the spider.

I remember one particular day when a tarantula was meandering down the middle of the street in front of our house. She screamed, grabbed her keys, ran to the car, backed out of the driveway, and ran over it. Through her actions in response to the sight of the tarantula, I learned to be afraid of big, hairy spiders.

After repeated exposure to her fearful behavior and resultant actions, it took only one or two more times of seeing a tarantula (anywhere around our home) for me to become afraid not just of tarantulas, but of all large brown spiders. Logically I know a big hairy spider won't hurt me. Yes, they're big, but they're not dangerous. I now have a very significant emotional response (a conditioned fear response) to the sight of a tarantula—even a photo of a big spider will make me close my eyes and shiver.

Today if I see a large brown house spider I'll squeal and run out of the room. I consider myself a pretty confident woman. It always frustrates the heck out of me when I run away because logically, I know the spider won't hurt me, but I cannot control my emotional response.

Once the emotion is installed, it's difficult to change. That's why it's important to consider the situations in which you put your dog so that as much as humanly possible, you create a happy emotional response for him.

Dog example:
As I described earlier, long before Brad and I were dog trainers, we took our dog Abbey to an old-fashioned obedience school that used choke collars, prong collars, and techniques that resulted in pain and fear for her. I wish I had known then what I know now. When we know better, we do better.

Abbey learned very quickly the training center wasn't fun. The moment we pulled into the parking lot and got out of the car, Abbey put her brakes on. She didn't even want to jump out of the car. We'd eventually coax her out only to watch her plant

Cold Nose College client dogs developed a happy emotional response to our training center because good stuff happened inside.

her four paws on the parking lot pavement and resist our tugs on the leash to move toward the door. It was an effort to get her inside. She developed an uncomfortable emotional response *to* the training center because of the pain and fear she experienced during training *in* the training center.

Contrast that to the myriad of dogs who trained in our Cold Nose College training center. As Brad and I were waiting for clients and dogs to come to class, we'd look out the training center windows and watch the dogs eagerly leading the way with their guardians behind them. These dogs learned that good stuff happened inside the training center, and they wanted more of that fun. These dogs developed a happy emotional response *to* our training center.

That's what you want for your dog during each recall training exercise—for him to develop a happy emotional response to every training moment.

Operant Conditioning

Consequences drive behavior. If the consequence of a given behavior works out to benefit of the dog, the behavior is likely to occur again. If there is no benefit to the dog, or if there is an unpleasant consequence, the behavior will likely decrease.

We can thank B. F. Skinner for helping us learn about operant conditioning. Skinner is thought of as the father of operant conditioning. Through this type of learning, a dog (or person) makes an association between a particular behavior and a consequence.

There are four processes of operant conditioning:

- Positive reinforcement
- Negative reinforcement

- Positive punishment
- Negative punishment

I want you to put on your scientist hat and think of positive and negative differently than you usually do—this time with a minus sign (-) or a plus sign (+). Alternatively, you could put on your accountant hat and think of positive and negative as it relates to balancing your checkbook. Positive (+) means money was added, negative (-) means money was subtracted or taken away.

When the word "positive" is used in learning theory, positive means something is added, and "negative" means something is taken away.

Now let's talk about reinforcement and punishment—reinforcement increases behavior and punishment decreases behavior.

Pat Miller of Peaceable Paws has a fantastic way of shedding light on each of these four processes:

- Positive reinforcement
  - Dog's behavior makes a good thing happen; behavior increases
- Positive punishment
  - Dog's behavior makes a bad thing happen; behavior decreases
- Negative reinforcement
  - Dog's behavior makes a bad thing go away; behavior increases
- Negative punishment
  - Dog's behavior makes a good thing go away; behavior decreases

Let's examine the processes one by one with example scenarios for both a dog and a human.

Positive Reinforcement

When using this process, something is added to cause a behavior to happen more frequently. An example: when a dog sits, the dog gets a yummy piece of food, and the behavior of sitting is

When you use positive reinforcement during training, your dog feels delighted during the learning process. Choose delight!

likely to increase (assuming the dog actually likes the piece of food). The reinforcer must be something the dog likes.

When I use positive reinforcement, my dog feels joyful in the learning process. I know this by watching the happy way her body moves and the bright look in her eyes. It's that same look of enjoyment my clients see in their own dogs when their dogs learn something new through the use of positive reinforcement. Happy human. Happy dog.

When I was a kid, my father, who had a PhD in clinical psychology and studied Skinner's work, used positive reinforcement to raise me. For every "A" I got on a report card, I was handed a $5 bill. Pretty darn reinforcing for me as a kid. That's a good bit of money today and certainly was way back then. I was definitely motivated to study more so that I would receive more As which in turn would earn me more $5 bills.

Humans can understand what behavior earned them reinforcement, even if there is a large time gap between the behavior and the consequence, such as my further studying to get more As. Our dogs do not, so that's why it's important to reinforce your dog the moment the behavior you like occurs, otherwise the dog may not make the connection with the behavior and the reinforcer.

Negative Reinforcement

When using negative reinforcement, something is removed in an attempt to increase a behavior. Sounds like something you might want—an increase in behavior, right?

Not so fast. The problem is what's removed is unpleasant to the dog, so something unpleasant must first be applied before it can be removed.

Choke collars and prong collars are examples of two training tools that fall in this area. When the dog displays a behavior the handler doesn't like, for example pulling on leash, the choke chain or prong collar is pulled tight and the discomfort of the tightened tool around the dog's neck causes the dog to stop pulling, in which case the handler slacks the leash, taking away the pain and discomfort of the prong collar around the neck. Walking nicely on a leash is more likely to happen. What does a dog feel when this type of training is used? Relief from the pain and discomfort.

My husband, Brad, tells a story that's a fine example of how negative reinforcement was used by his paternal grandmother to get him to sit quietly in a chair. When he and his brother were getting a bit too rowdy, she'd walk over to him, pinch his ear tightly and lead him to a chair. That ear pinch hurt! When he sat down, she'd release the ear pinch. His behavior of sitting in the chair increased. I'm not suggesting you try this with your child, but it's a fine example of negative reinforcement, a training technique that's not in my toolkit.

While I don't use negative reinforcement for training recall or family manners, other professional trainers use it effectively for behavior modification. Constructional Aggression Treatment (CAT) is a technique where a dog is exposed to a trigger (while keeping the dog below his stress threshold), waiting for the dog to offer an alternative behavior, and then reinforcing the dog by removing the trigger. So negative reinforcement can be used beneficially, but not something you'll use for recall training.

Positive Punishment

You still have on your scientist hat, yes? Positive means something is added. So when one uses positive punishment, something is added in an attempt to decrease a behavior. I do not use, nor do I recommend you use positive punishment. Positive punishment can work, but its use comes with many unintended consequences.

For example, a person sprays water in the dog's face for doing something the person doesn't like in an attempt to decrease the unwanted behavior (no, I'm not suggesting you do this). The water in the face may stop the behavior (though I suspect it only interrupts the dog from performing the unwanted behavior in the moment), yet hasn't taught the dog what *to do*. In the absence of the person who doled out the punishment, the dog will likely still perform the unwanted behavior.

An example of positive punishment is when a person scolds their dog for getting on the couch or in the trash. The dog may learn to stay off the couch or out of the trash when the person is present, but when the person is away, all bets are off. I know this to be true.

Long before I became a dog trainer, I didn't want Abbey, our first dog, to sleep on our bed while we were away, so I scolded her every time I saw her on the bed or she attempted to jump up on the bed. It wasn't long before she stayed off the bed when I was home. Interestingly enough, when I came home after a day at work, she'd waltz out of our bedroom. I suspected she just jumped off the bed. My suspicions were confirmed by feeling the bedquilt. Sure enough, body heat.

I must say that now I don't mind if my dogs choose to sleep on the bed whether or not I'm home and I adore having my dogs sleep with me. It's just another soft place we both enjoy together.

Another example of positive punishment is the use of

choke collars and prong collars—still used by some handlers to decrease a dog's behavior of pulling on leash. The dog pulls and the handler gives a collar correction, which means pain is applied (added). In this case, the dog's behavior made a bad thing happen, and the behavior of pulling on leash decreases (no, I don't suggest you do this).

I've always enjoyed the way Pat Miller of Peaceable Paws and Steve White of ProActive K9 refer to the risks and challenges of using positive punishment, which is adding something in an attempt to stop an unwanted behavior.

Steve White's Nine Rules for Using Punishment

1. It must be something the dog will work to avoid.
    This is a subjective experience unique to the individual.
2. It must be unexpected.
    Knowing it's coming can change the behavioral economics of the event.
3. It must suppress behavior.
    Aversives applied without effect basically constitute abuse.
4. It must be of the perfect intensity.
    Too much and the subject bails; too little a punishment callus develops.
5. It must happen immediately.
    Otherwise you risk punishing subsequent behaviors.
6. It must be associated with the behavior, not you or the delivery mechanism.
    Far too many of us are the discriminative stimuli that punishment is at hand.
7. It must happen every time the behavior occurs.

Otherwise we strengthen problem behavior with a random reinforcement schedule.

8. There must be an alternative for the dog.
   Make the contrast clear between the paths to reinforcement or punishment.

9. Never forget punishment reinforces the individual punishing.
   This insidious effect happens just because you get momentary relief from annoyance.

One final thought: if you are tempted to use punishment and cannot follow all these guidelines then *you should rethink your training plan.*

Pat Miller's 12 Pitfalls of Positive Punishment

1. You can cause physical pain/damage to your dog.
2. It is difficult to gauge the appropriate intensity.
3. The dog can develop a "punishment callus."
4. The behavior may return when punishment stops.
5. It is difficult to have perfect timing.
6. It is difficult to be perfectly consistent.
7. It can suppress desired behaviors; inhibit offered behaviors.
8. It doesn't teach the dog what to do.
9. The suppressive effect of the punisher is limited to the presence of the discriminative stimuli.
10. It is rewarding to the punisher.
11. It can damage the dog's confidence, trust in the trainer, relationship between dog and human.
12. Violence begets violence.

There are many serious, unintended consequences when using positive punishment, one of which is the loss of trust. I want my dog to trust me. I don't want her wondering, "Is this the nice person today or the scary person?"

In this book you'll be learning a recall training methodology that uses positive reinforcement to train your dog to come.

Negative Punishment

This principle of operant conditioning is one that's sometimes used in modern, humane dog training. Does that sound odd to you? Punishment in force-free training?

Remember that negative means something is removed. In the case of a dog jumping up, something the dog likes is removed to reduce the dog's unwanted behavior. Withdrawing attention from a dog who jumps up on people is considered negative punishment. The attention is taken away (negative) to reduce the jumping. Yet as soon as all four paws are on the ground if you give the dog attention or a treat, you've added (positive) something to increase (reinforcement) the likelihood that the dog will keep his paws on the floor when greeting a person.

Quickly closing the door when a dog tries to dart out is another example of negative punishment. The good thing—the opportunity to be out of doors—is taken away. I suggest using negative punishment sparingly. When and if you do, as soon as the dog offers the desired behavior, positively reinforce it.

I remember a time my dad used negative punishment on me when I was a teenager. I snuck off with a boy. When he found out about it, I was grounded and not permitted to attend afterschool or evening outings—all the fun things I loved. He took the good stuff away from me. I enjoyed my parents, so hanging out with them at home wasn't necessarily unpleasant, but this particular time the two-week grounding caused me to miss a really big rock and roll concert. I was devastated! I never snuck off with a boy again.

Learning Theory Is Always in Play

Ok, did I make your eyes glaze over? Are you still with me? You're likely wondering why all of this is important to you and your dog.

If you take the time to grasp a bit of learning theory, you'll be able to solve common training issues you're bound to encounter and will gain an understanding of the most effective method for training your dog (hint, hint, positive reinforcement!).

Keep in mind that consequences drive behavior. Once you begin understanding operant conditioning, you may find yourself exploring reasons for changes in your own behavior. I know I certainly do.

Here's an example of my own change in behavior that puzzled me. A few years ago we bought a pre-owned car that was newer than any car we previously owned. When the new car was moving without seatbelts fastened, the car would beep loudly. In the old car, I developed the habit of removing my seatbelt just as I was turning into the driveway. In the new car, the moment I unfastened my seat belt, a loud beeping noise started and continued until the seat belt was refastened or the car came to a stop. I really disliked that sound! It wasn't long before I started waiting for the car to come to a full stop before I took off my seat belt—I learned to keep my seat belt on. My behavior changed. Was something reinforcing to me or was something punishing to me? Was something added or was something taken away? I'll let you ponder that since you now understand learning by consequence.

Learning theory "is" just as gravity "is." It exists and though you may not fully understand it, it's in play every day with your dog (and you too).

If you take the time to understand classical conditioning and the four processes of operant conditioning, you'll have an even greater appreciation for how effective and enjoyable it can be to train your dog. Happy dog. Happy human.

Know Your ABCs:
Antecedent, Behavior, Consequence

I HOPE YOU'LL BECOME a master of arranging antecedents—the conditions present before the behavior your dog displays. But first, you must understand the ABCs as they're used in dog training.

The ABCs of Training

We have Edward Thorndike (1874–1949) to thank for teaching us about The Law of Effect. While studying behaviorism, he discovered The Law of Effect, which states that behaviors change as a result of the consequences to actions. Boundless Psychology's Lumen Learning course has a nice succinct explanation of The Law of Effect:

- "The Law of Effect states that responses that produce a satisfying effect in a particular situation become more likely to occur again in that situation, and responses

that produce a discomforting effect become less likely
to occur again in that situation.

- Thorndike is the psychologist who first studied the Law
  of Effect by placing hungry cats inside puzzle boxes and
  observing their actions. He quickly realized that cats
  could learn the efficacy of certain behaviors and would
  repeat those behaviors that allowed them to escape faster.

- The Law of Effect is at work in every human behavior
  as well. From a young age, we learn which actions are
  beneficial and which are detrimental through a similar
  trial and error process." (Lumen, n.d.)

So what is an antecedent? Technically, antecedents are the
conditions present prior to the behavior. In a training environment, some examples of antecedents are the environment itself,
a food lure, a physical prompt, a verbal cue, or a hand signal.

After the antecedent, you have the behavior (a recall, sit or
down), followed by the consequence of the behavior.

While the antecedent *prompted* the behavior to happen, it's
the *consequence* of the behavior that will cause the behavior to
happen more or less frequently.

Behaviors that are reinforced will be repeated, even if they're
unwanted behaviors. Remember to think about training from
the dog's perspective. What's in it for the dog? Will the consequence be more likely to increase or decrease the behavior?
Keeping the consequence in mind is a great way to problem
solve unwanted behaviors.

If your dog is counter surfing, what's in for him? You left a sandwich on the counter (antecedent), the dog jumped up and placed front paws on the counter (behavior), and the dog ate the sandwich (consequence). Because the dog surely enjoyed the sandwich, the behavior of jumping up on the counter is more likely to increase because it was reinforced.

"If you've got murky behavior it's because of unclear antecedents or consequences—or both. Clean up antecedents and consequences, and the behavior takes care of itself." ~ Steve White

Here's a simple way to think about the ABCs:

- Antecedents are the contributing factors to your dog's behavior.
- Behavior is the response your dog has as a result of the antecedent.
- Consequence is what happens after the dog's behavior that makes it more or less likely to happen again.

You can manipulate antecedents in a way that helps your dog achieve a desired behavior so it can be reinforced—making the behavior more likely to happen again.

An example of ineffective antecedent arrangement:
You believe your dog is ready to move from indoor to outdoor recall training practice. You grab some kibble and head outside to train in the front yard and your dog follows you. Just as you call your dog to come, a squirrel runs past, and off goes your dog in chase of the furry creature. You lost the opportunity to reinforce your dog for the behavior of returning to you when you called, and instead, he was reinforced by the opportunity to chase the squirrel. The consequence of chasing the squirrel (chasing is inherently reinforcing), makes the behavior of coming to you less likely.

Contrast the above scenario to this effective antecedent arrangement:
You believe your dog is ready to move from indoor to outdoor recall training practice. You put on a wearable treat bag filled with high-value treats and with your dog on a leash, you position yourself in the front yard. Just as you're about to call your dog to come, a squirrel runs by. Your dog notices the squirrel, pulls to the end of the leash, but the chase is prevented. Once the squirrel is past and your dog looks back at you, you call him to come—he does and you give him a high-value treat. The consequence of returning to you and eating a high-value treat makes the behavior of coming to you more likely to happen again.

I enjoy Steve White's comment about the ABCs, *"If you've got murky behavior it's because of unclear antecedents or consequences—or both. Clean up antecedents and consequences, and the behavior takes care of itself."*

[6]

Be Aware:
Potential Speed Bumps Ahead

WHEN TEACHING YOUR DOG something new, there will always be peaks and valleys during the learning journey—even when you do everything right. Obstacles are bound to occur, yet it's how we handle those obstacles that causes one person to falter and another to move on to success.

As you implement the training techniques I recommend, you'll likely encounter a few speed bumps along the way. You'll need to reach for your problem-solving hat. If you're aware of challenges that can occur, it'll be easier to understand and figure out what to change to bring about success.

Here are a few reasons speed bumps pop up:

- Failure to choose a reinforcer that's high enough in value
- Lack of understanding of how to add distance, duration, and distractions to training exercises
- Extraneous body movement when training

Don't be discouraged if you encounter a training speed bump during recall training. Even when you do everything right, there will always be peaks and valleys during the learning journey.

- Lack of clarity about what you're training
- Frustration during learning (yours and your dog's)
- Negative frame of mind
- Training when your dog isn't well
- Failure to back up in training when an exercise doesn't bring about success

Choosing Food and the Value of Reinforcers
You'll be using food to reinforce your dog during training exercises. Think of food as your dog's paycheck.

The type of food you choose should be something your dog loves and doesn't receive daily. I sometimes use pre-packaged treats made for dogs or my dog's kibble, but I also use human food I happen to have available in our house or can get from the grocery store.

Dogs have different preferences, just as we do. A food one dog likes may not please another, so experiment to find the types of food your dog loves—operative word, *loves*.

Does he love it (he can't wait to get another piece)? Is it just so-so (he takes the food and then wanders off)? Does he turn up his nose at the food as if saying, "No way, I'm gonna eat that!"? As you're experimenting with different foods, think in terms of ranking your dog's preferences as low, medium, or high-value food.

Over the years I learned from experience most dogs find hot dogs, baked or grilled meat (chicken, pork, beef), cheese (the stinkier, the better), Vienna sausages, liverwurst, canned chicken or tuna, and Spam to be irresistible. In our Rocket Recall two-day workshops we offered a wide variety of foods for students to try with their dogs. You can do the same—experiment to find foods your dog will do back-flips for and use that food during recall training exercises. Merely switching to a higher value food can dramatically increase your dog's interest and the success of a training exercise.

As you progress in the training exercises in this book, you may choose to use toys (instead of food) to reinforce your dog for returning to you. Each dog has toy preferences, so choose a toy that your dog finds exciting. You'll learn more about the variety of reinforcers available to you in the next chapter.

The Three Ds: Distance, Duration, and Distractions

Understanding the Three Ds and how to use them is like having the keys to the kingdom: you'll possess profound knowledge.

Your dog will stay focused on you when you strategically add distance, duration, and distractions into a training plan. Each component should be introduced one at a time—otherwise, your dog has difficulty achieving the task at hand.

Distance is how far away you are from your dog when you call him.

Distance is how far away you are from your dog when you call him. Is he one foot away, twenty feet away, or fifty feet away from you? You'll begin training with very little distance between you and your dog. As you progress, you'll gradually increase distance. Only when you have achieved some degree of distance, will you add in a distraction.

I began training Cailie to come to me with only three feet between us. We started in the house and she was on leash. Only when I achieved success with distance did I begin training with our multiple cats in the same room (a distraction).

Duration is the length of time the dog holds a position. When teaching a dog to wait, duration is the length of time the dog remains in place until you release him. When you're ready to extend duration, you'll lessen the distance *and* lower the distractions in the environment.

In recall training, your dog isn't holding a position. Yet when your dog is running to you from some distance, duration is involved because the dog must continue to travel from Point A (where he was) to Point B (where you're standing) without losing focus on you.

Duration is the length of time the dog holds a position. Duration is involved when training recall because the dog must continue to travel from where he was to where you're standing without losing focus on you.

Distractions are things in the training environment that cause your dog to lose focus on you—a squirrel, a leaf blowing in the wind, a passerby, another dog, a cat, or children playing nearby. The distance from the distraction or the intensity of a distraction can positively or negatively affect a dog's success during training.

Let's say I want to practice recall training at the community park. I arrive to find a softball game in progress, and the rowdy crowd in the bleachers is cheering. The intensity of the sound (the loud cheers) would impact my training—no doubt Cailie would be distracted. Because my goal is for her to be successful in coming to me when called, I'll begin practicing recall some distance away from the ball field—far enough that she can focus on me. To ensure the sounds of the crowd don't negatively affect her success, I may need to choose a spot out of sight of the field. In this example, I increased the distance from the distraction (the ball field) and lowered the intensity of the distraction (the cheering crowd) to set Cailie up for success.

Keeping the Three Ds in mind and strategically adding

them into training will help you achieve training goals.

Your Body Language

Dogs are masters at reading our body language. No doubt you've noticed that your dog seems to know what you're going to do before you do it. The

Distractions are things in the training environment that cause your dog to lose focus on you.

slightest movement of my hand toward the drawer where postage stamps are kept will cause Cailie to run to my side in anticipation of a trip to the mailbox. Yes, I still mail letters—albeit infrequently.

In another chapter, you'll learn about clean training mechanics. This means the way you use your body (or parts of your body) during a training session. Dogs are keen observers—meaning they observe our every move. Your dog could become dependent on a body movement that you're not aware of doing. You might think he's responding to your verbal cue when he's really responding to your body movement.

Generally speaking, less body movement means your dog has a better chance of learning what you're teaching. Minimize body movement so you don't distract your dog from the task at hand.

Be Clear about What You're Asking

Cailie is a quick learner when I'm clear about my goals. I've confused her when I didn't plan a training session and instead just launched into training. I'm human—it happens.

Take the time to create a training plan, or better yet, write it out. A written training plan provides clarity. And clarity helps set your dog up for success so that you reach your goal.

Frustration During Training—Yours and Your Dog's

It's normal to feel frustrated when learning something new. I've been frustrated while practicing the banjo to improve my skill. Frustration occurs when I start judging my progress. I'm putting in the work, yet there are times when I'm not making progress—I've reached a plateau in learning. Because I understand learning doesn't occur in a straight line, I stop, take a deep breath, and realize that with continued time on the instrument, I'll eventually begin making forward progress.

One way to prevent your own frustration during training is to get rid of expectations. When expectations don't match reality, it's easy to get frustrated.

Standing in the checkout line at the grocery store is an example of how frustration can occur. You might be frustrated that it's taking longer than it should at check out. But the reality is that it's taking a long time—several people are ahead of you, all with full grocery carts. Your expectation is that the line *should* move faster. The reality is that the line is moving slowly. Your expectation doesn't line up with reality. The fact—moving through the checkout line will take *as long as it takes*. What's the solution? Throw out your expectations (and take a deep breath).

Your dog may get frustrated too. Even when you do everything right, the mere fact that he's learning something new can lead to frustration.

If your dog is disengaging with you during a training session, it's time to take a break. Play tug or a quick game of fetch. While you're playing, consider your training goal for that session. What occurred? How might you tweak your plan to help to reengage him so he achieves your intended goal? Come up with answers and try again. Your try will likely be met with success. If not, end the training session with something your dog knows how to do—ask for a sit, reinforce it, and call it a day.

Your Frame of Mind

When you're happy and smiling, your dog notices and will feel happier during training. We all have days when we feel like curmudgeons, but no one wants to work with a crabby training partner, not even your dog.

You may choose to do what I do. When feeling out of sorts, I may skip training for the day. But other times, I launch into a training session with Cailie because it raises my spirits. How can I not find joy looking into her amber eyes and noticing her exuberance during training? Yet if I start a training session and my psyche doesn't improve, I merely end our training session with something she enjoys—a game of tug, a puzzle toy, or scattering food in her snuffle mat.

The Health of Your Dog

There are times when you know your dog isn't well. Maybe your dog sprained a muscle, is recovering from surgery, or has a minor infection. Less than optimal health impedes learning.

Hiding pain is something dogs do well and is an evolutionary trait. In the wild, a dog who shows pain (or appears weak) has a lower chance of survival. Your dog may be in pain and not show it. If attempts to engage your dog in training are frequently met with lackluster behavior, a veterinary consult may be needed to rule out medical issues.

When you know your dog isn't well, set recall training aside. In fact, you may choose to set all training aside until your dog is well.

Return to the Point of Last Success

You're learning a systematic and progressive method of training recall. It's human nature to want to reach your goal quickly, yet your dog learns at his own pace. The exercises are designed to be taught and practiced in succession. Try not to rush the process.

You're bound to reach points where you do everything I suggest, yet your dog just doesn't get it. Don't worry. There is individuality in learning. Merely return to the exercise where your dog was last successful and stay at that point for a day or two before moving forward, and your efforts will likely be met with rousing success.

Management:
What It Is and Why It's Important

TO UNDERSTAND why management is important, you first have to understand the definition as it's used in the animal training world.

Management means manipulating the dog's environment to prevent the dog from practicing and being reinforced for an unwanted behavior (running away from you when you call him) while training an alternative behavior (an immediate return to you when you call).

The techniques in this book will teach you how to train your dog to come to you, but I want you to also learn why management is important. In the world of dog training "management and training" comprise the quintessential dynamic duo.

Dog trainers always develop a management strategy during the training process, and you'd be wise to do so too.

Examples of Management

Here are two general examples of how you can use management to prevent reinforcement for an unwanted behavior while you're training a behavior you prefer your dog to do.

The Counter Surfer

If your dog is counter surfing, I'd lay money on the fact that he periodically gets something desirable off the counter. Grabbing that leftover piece of a sandwich is reinforcing to the dog. Jumping up on the counter is reinforced by the dog gaining access to and eating the piece of sandwich. Reinforcement is what makes a behavior more likely to occur again, so your sweet dog will make the move again because it worked for him the first time. Management to the rescue.

The management strategy for counter surfing is to keep all counters clear of anything that might be tempting to the dog.

1) Grabbing something tasty off a counter is reinforcing to the dog. 2) The management strategy for counter surfing is to keep all counters clear of anything that might be tempting to the dog.

That means food, paper products, anything and everything that the dog might be tempted to reach and pull down with his mouth or paws. Once the counters are clear of those delectable items, then the training plan would be to generously and consistently reinforce the dog with a yummy treat for keeping four feet on the floor while he's in the kitchen or perhaps even reinforce him by tossing treats to him when he's standing or sitting at the entrance to the kitchen.

The Tissue Thief

Years ago a client called and asked me to teach her dog to stay out of the bathroom trash can. Each time he walked into the bathroom he helped himself to the dirty tissues in the can. While I was capable of creating an effective training plan to help the dog learn to stay out of the can, I suggested to her it would be easier to merely put the lid on the bathroom trash can. Voila! Problem solved. The dog was no longer able to grab tissues from the trash can. No training plan was needed and no money was spent on training. This is a perfect example of how management can be an easy fix.

Management Sets the Dog Up for Success

But what does that mean and why? Setting a dog up for success in recall training prevents the dog from being reinforced for the behavior you don't want (running away from you) while training him to do what you *do* want (coming quickly to you).

A sound management strategy ensures your dog will be reinforced for the *wanted* behavior of coming to you. Remember what you learned in the Understanding How Dogs Learn chap-

With your dog on a leash, you can be certain he's not going to run away to sniff an odor or chase a squirrel. Instead, he'll come to you.

ter? Reinforcement increases the probability the behavior will happen again.

Think about reinforcement from the dog's perspective (you'll learn reinforcement strategies in the next chapter). If you call your dog to come and he runs the other way, he's getting reinforced by the opportunity to stay out of doors, by sniffing all sorts of wonderful smells, and maybe even by taking a swim in a nearby lake. All those things are valuable (reinforcing) to him, which means he may be less likely to respond to your call when there are other interesting things available.

Your goal during recall training is to prevent your dog from running away from you while training him to turn on a dime and return to you.

So what's the management strategy for training a recall? A leash.

When you first start training recall, you'll use a 6-foot leash, then graduate to a 15-to-20-foot leash until you have some degree of success before you start off-leash training.

With your dog on a leash, you can be certain he's not going to run away to sniff an odor or chase a squirrel. Instead, he'll come to you.

[8]

The Importance of Reinforcers

WHAT IS A REINFORCER?

A reinforcer is a stimulus (something the dog likes) that increases the chance of a desired response (when given after the response).

Think about reinforcement from the learner's perspective. When training recall, your dog is the learner. What is it that he will find reinforcing?

Experiment and identify a food he finds beyond delicious. Not all dogs like the same types of foods. Just because it's a meat product doesn't mean a dog will love it and just because it's a vegetable product, it doesn't mean your dog won't like it. I've had dogs spit out a hot dog and prefer a carrot.

Here's a human example, I love cottage cheese. If you asked me to perform a simple job for you, a bowl of cottage cheese would be reinforcing to me. My husband, Brad, hates cottage cheese. You could chase him out of the room by holding a teaspoon of cottage cheese and walking toward him. Seriously, that's true. What's reinforcing to me isn't always reinforcing to him.

Primary and Secondary Reinforcers

Let me share a little bit about primary and secondary reinforcers. Understanding the difference will help you choose the most appropriate reinforcer for your own dog during the different phases of your training journey.

Primary reinforcers are things that have innate value to the dog, meaning they don't have to be learned, such as water, food, safety, and sleep.

Secondary reinforcers are things a dog has learned to value because of the pairing with a primary reinforcer. For example, the sound of a marker signal (clicker or verbal marker) takes on value because it has been paired with food.

When training recall, you'll first choose food to reinforce your dog because it's a primary reinforcer. Over time you may choose to move to secondary reinforcers, such as playing tug—assuming your dog enjoys tug (some dogs do not).

Reinforcers, Distance, and Distractions

The appropriate pairing of reinforcers with distance and distractions is the key to successful training.

You'll learn to call your dog from varying distances and away from a variety of distractions.

A distraction is anything that takes your dog's attention away from you. Distractions can be as simple as a leaf falling from a tree that causes your dog to look away momentarily or a stray cat running through your yard that causes your dog to bolt toward the cat. I suspect you know your dog quite well, so you're aware of the myriad of things that cause your dog to lose focus on you.

Distance also comes into play. It's important to consider the distance your dog will need to travel to return to you when you call him (even without a distraction present). A longer distance recall is more challenging for the dog than a short distance recall. It's easier for Cailie to return to me when she's ten feet away than it is to come to me from the back of our pasture—a distance of about 250 yards.

Think of reinforcement as your dog's paycheck. Different jobs require different paychecks. I like to pay well for succeeding with challenging work. Because each dog values a specific reinforcer differently, experiment to find out which foods or other reinforcers your dog really likes. Be creative!

If I call Cailie and she turns on a dime and comes running to me from the far side of our seven-acre pasture (a long distance) with the scent of deer nearby (a distraction), you can be sure I'll reinforce her with a portion of food she'll do backflips over. Distance coupled with a distraction ratchets up the difficulty.

On the other hand, if we're both in the house and I call her from another room (a short distance with lesser distractions than outside) and she comes running to me when I call her, a piece of kibble would be an appropriate paycheck for the easier job.

However, if she's only a few feet away from me but looking at a squirrel on the ground when I call and she turns to me immediately, I'm going to pay her well for the hard work of coming to me in the midst of a big distraction—the squirrel.

In essence, short distances and low distractions can be paired with low-value reinforcers and longer distances and high distractions should be paired with high-value reinforcers.

As you choose different values of foods to have ready for easy reinforcement, be sure to keep low-, medium-, and high-value foods separate from one another (resist the temptation to mix different values of food in one bag). Keeping them separate allows you to intelligently decide when to raise or lower the value of the reinforcer.

But how do you know if the food you're using is valuable enough for your dog? When you deliver a reinforcer to your dog, he should eagerly move toward you for another piece of food as if to say "OMG, that was good! I'd like another, please."

[9]

Create a Reinforcement Hierarchy

CREATING A REINFORCEMENT HIERARCHY will help you understand how your dog views his world. What's important to him? What is distracting to him?

To build a written reinforcement hierarchy begin by identifying twenty to thirty reinforcers (foods, toys, and other things your dog loves) and rank those as low, medium, or high value. Then identify twenty to thirty distractions (another dog, a squirrel, a leaf blowing in the wind) and rank those as low, medium, or high level.

Keep in mind that something that's distracting to your dog may also be reinforcing. Reinforcers and distractions can overlap. A pond or creek can be distracting to Cailie, but because she loves swimming, the same pond or creek can also be reinforcing.

As you consider reinforcers for your dog, think beyond what you feed your dog when training. If you're out walking with your dog and he's eagerly pulling to get to another dog to visit, the opportunity to greet another dog is reinforcing to him.

Once you have your list of reinforcers and distractions, it's time for pairing. Your next step is to look at each list and pair the low-level distractions with low-value reinforcers, the medium-level distractions with the medium-value reinforcers, and the high-level distractions with high-value reinforcers.

Cailie's Reinforcers

Happy Howie's treats
Banana
Cheese
Hot dogs
Freeze-dried salmon
Greeting a dog
Greeting a person
Playing with a flirt pole
Steak
Meatballs
Playing tug
Playing with her brother Cody
Swimming
Chasing a Jolly Ball
Chasing water from a hose
Greeting a child
Baked chicken
Chasing a squirrel
Dried banana chips
Deer poop
Playing with a Chuckit! Ball
Digging

Dried cat food
Being cued for an established behavior
Kibble
Peanut butter
Being praised
Wet cat food
Chasing a Kong Wubba
Kissing Brad

Notice I listed a variety of things Cailie finds reinforcing. Not all of them would I choose as a reinforcer to pay her for a job well done, but they *are* reinforcing to her (yes, she will eat deer poop in a nanosecond). Some items that are reinforcing also end up being a distraction.

Cailie's Distractions

A dog
A person
A UPS truck
Brad
A river
A lake
A cat sitting still
A moving squirrel
A child
Deer poop
Deer grazing in a pasture
Handler movement
An open door

A blowing leaf
Scent on the ground
A cat litter box
Kibble on the floor
A standup paddleboard
A water toy
A parked car in the driveway
A moving cat
The sound of a tractor
The sight of a tractor
A low-flying bird
Her brother Cody
A car pulling in the driveway
A person walking by the house
A Kong Wubba
A Jolly Ball
The scent of a rabbit

Again, notice some things I listed are also on the reinforcer list. In the right setting and with safety in mind, you can reinforce your dog with something that is also placed on the distraction list. For example, a lake is distracting to Cailie because she loves to swim. If there's a lake near where I'm training, she'll have a more difficult time focusing on me; but if I were in a safe location and wanted to reinforce her for a rocket-like recall, I could then cue her to "go swim" and the opportunity to swim would be highly reinforcing to her. Swimming would reinforce her return to me.

My Ranking of Cailie's Reinforcers

<u>Low-Value Reinforcers</u>
Happy Howie's treats
Banana
Playing with her brother Cody
Dried banana chips
Dried cat food
Being cued for an established behavior
Kibble
Being praised

<u>Medium-Value Reinforcers</u>
Cheese
Hot dogs
Steak
Meatballs
Playing tug
Swimming
Baked chicken
Digging
Wet cat food
Chasing a Kong Wubba
Kissing Brad

<u>High-Value Reinforcers</u>
Freeze-dried salmon
Greeting a dog
Greeting a person
Playing with a flirt pole

Chasing a Jolly Ball
Chasing water from a hose
Greeting a child
Chasing a squirrel
Deer poop
Playing with a Chuckit! ball
Peanut butter

My Ranking of Cailie's Distractions

<u>Low-Level Distractions</u>
A cat sitting still
Handler movement
An open door
A blowing leaf
Kibble on the floor
A low-flying bird

If you refer back to Cailie's entire list of distractions I shared earlier, I listed thirty distractions. Looking at the short list of only six low-level distractions you can surmise that with so few low-level distractions, she's an easily distracted dog.

Take another look at your lists of distractions. Is your dog also easily distracted? If so, no worries—you're learning how to pair distractions with the appropriate value reinforcers.

<u>Medium-Level Distractions</u>
A dog
A person

Brad
A river
A lake
A child
Deer grazing in a pasture
A cat litter box
A standup paddleboard
A water toy
A moving cat
Her brother Cody
A Kong Wubba

High-Level Distractions
A UPS truck
A moving squirrel
Deer poop
Scent on the ground
A parked car in the driveway
The sound of a tractor
The sight of a moving tractor
A car pulling into the driveway
A person walking by the house
A Jolly Ball
The scent of a rabbit

When I first put the distraction lists together for Cailie, it confirmed what I already knew—many things distracted her. Even though I knew she was easily distracted, by looking at the list I gained further insight as to how to use the right level of reinforcer while training in the presence of distractions.

Cailie notices everything in her environment and while all dogs see the world through their olfactory system, you'd think my Australian Shepherd is a hound. The scent of prey is highly distracing to her—especially rabbit scent.

Pairing Distractions with Reinforcers

After I considered each item listed on the distraction and re-inforcer lists, I paired Cailie's distractions and reinforcers. I thought about the distraction then chose a reinforcer I felt she would be willing to recall for in the presence of the specific distraction.

When distractions and reinforcers are paired appropriately, your dog's focus and your own training efforts succeed.

For recall training be successful, I strive to pick the reinforcer she'll be excited to work for when training in the presence of the particular level of distraction.

While the lists below show the pairing of specific distractions and reinforcers (for example handler movement is paired with banana) I can use any one of Cailie's low-value reinforcers when training recall amid low-level distractions. Instead of banana, dried cat food would also be appropriate.

Low-Level Distractions Paired with Low-Value Reinforcers

A cat sitting still	Happy Howie's treats
Handler movement	Banana
An open door	Playing with Cody
A blowing leaf	Dried banana chips
Kibble on the floor	Dried cat food
A low-flying bird	Cue for established behavior
Kibble	
Praise	

When training at home with our cat sitting nearby, theoretically I should be able to use any one of the listed low-value reinforcers to pay Cailie for returning to me when I call her. I say theoretically because you should always be prepared to raise the value of the reinforcer if your dog isn't eagerly engaged and giving you the "OMG, I want another piece!" look.

Anytime I'm training my dog, and something doesn't go the way I anticipate, it's good information for me. I take a pause and consider the distractions in the environment, the value of my renforcer, and how my dog may be feeling in that moment.

Medium-Level Distractions
Paired with Medium-Value Reinforcers

A dog	Cheese
A person	Hot dogs
Brad	Steak
A river	Meatballs
A lake	Playing tug
A child	Swimming
Deer grazing in a pasture	Baked chicken
A cat litter box	Digging
A standup paddleboard	Wet cat food
A water toy	Chasing a Kong Wubba
A moving cat	Kissing Brad

On this list did you notice the Brad is listed as a distraction and also as a reinforcer? When I'm training Cailie and he walks into the room, she'll definitely be distracted by his presence. To take her attention away from him, I can cue her to perform a known behavior such as "look at me" followed by the opportunity to go slather Brad in kisses. I actually have kissing Brad on a verbal cue, "Go give Brad kisses."

High-Level Distractions Paired with High-Value Reinforcers

UPS truck	Freeze-dried salmon
A moving squirrel	Greeting a dog
Deer poop	Greeting a person
Scent on the ground	Playing with a flirt pole
A car in the driveway	Chasing a Jolly Ball

The sound of a tractor	Chasing water from a hose
The sight of a moving tractor	Greeting a child
A car pulling into driveway	Chasing a squirrel
A person walking by the house	Freeze-dried salmon
A Jolly Ball	A Chuckit! ball
The scent of a rabbit	A Chuckit! ball

While some of the reinforcers I listed aren't always readily available to use during Rocket Recall training, such as chasing water from a hose, I can use that activity during other training sessions (even if it's impromptu training) because I know it's highly reinforcing to Cailie. She's very distracted when I water the garden and tries to bite the water coming out of the hose. I cue her to sit and wait while I water a few plants, then release her to chase the water from the hose. Chasing the water reinforces her behavior of sitting and waiting. Chasing water is another example of a distraction that's also a reinforcer.

Notice the above list shows the Jolly Ball as a distraction and also as a reinforcer. The scent of a rabbit is highly distracting for Cailie. When she has her nose to the ground following a rabbit scent, and I cue her to look at me, when she turns to look I can throw the Jolly Ball for her to play with to reinforce the fact that she left the rabbit scent—a big deal!

If distractions and reinforcers are paired inappropriately, your dog's focus and your training suffer, but if paired wisely, everyone succeeds.

[10]

Marker Training

MARKER TRAINING is a popular method of dog training that enhances communication with a dog. It incorporates a sound or other signal that *marks* a desired behavior of the dog and becomes a communication tool to help him understand what will earn him reinforcement.

The marker also bridges the gap between the time the behavior happens and the time the reinforcer is delivered to the dog. In the simplest explanation, it's a signal that tells the dog when his action will pay off.

This style of training was developed by Keller Breland, Marian Breland Bailey, and Bob Bailey in the 1960s and was used in marine mammal training. The dog training world has Karen Pryor to thank for popularizing the use of marker training.

I have several different marker signals I use at different times with Cailie: the sound of a clicker (a small plastic device with metal inside), a verbal sound (Yes or Yip), and a palatal click, the sound made when I touch the tip of my tongue to the roof of my mouth and release the pressure between the two—the sound resembles a pop. Here's how to do the palatal click, also known as a tongue click: place the tip of your tongue on the roof of your mouth and slightly behind your upper teeth, but ahead of the point where the roof of your mouth begins to curve. With tongue pressure against the roof of your mouth, quickly draw your tongue downwards as you open your mouth. The pressure against the roof of your mouth, coupled with the quick removal of your tongue, creates a popping sound.

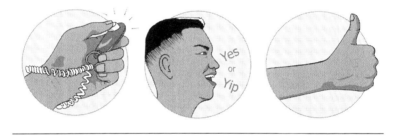

A marker is a signal that tells the dog when his action will pay off. Marker signal examples: the sound of a clicker, a verbal sound, or a thumbs-up gesture for a deaf dog.

The use of marker training is effective for any dog, young or old, or even blind or deaf dogs. You can use a visual signal (thumbs-up gesture or flick of the hand for a deaf dog—we use the thumbs-up gesture for our dog, Cody, who has acquired deafness). For a dog both deaf and blind, it could be a light tap to the shoulder.

It's important to understand a marker signal must always be followed by a reinforcer, preferably food (it's a primary reinforcer). Even if you mark by mistake, your dog still gets the food. Marking without feeding is akin to your paycheck bouncing. If you were paid for a job well done but your paycheck bounced, I suspect you'd think twice about going back to work. Your behavior of *going to work* would diminish. You want to preserve your dog's trust in the marker training system, so pay your dog even if you mark by mistake.

Marker training teaches a dog what to do and creates an enthusiastic learner because the sound is followed by positive reinforcement. Think back to what you learned earlier about positive reinforcement—positive means something is added to strengthen a behavior. The dog is motivated to continue working to earn reinforcement. I never fail to see enthusiasm and joy in my dog's eyes when we're training.

Pairing the marker sound with something the dog likes, such as a yummy piece of food, creates a happy association between the marker signal and the food. The dog quickly learns the marker sound means he'll get the treat. I call this "turning on the marker." You'll learn how to Turn on the Marker in the Clean Training Skills section.

Marking and Training Skills

Learning to use clear, clean body language and effective marking skills during training sessions will speed up your dog's learning.

How you use your body, arms, and hands during a training session can enhance or detract from your dog's success. Dogs are experts at reading human body language and notice our every move. Extraneous body movement can be construed by the dog as vitally important to the training at hand, when it's merely your own habit of moving during training. If there's too much extraneous movement it will confuse the dog.

Clean Marking Skills

The marker signal you select should be as clear and consistent as possible.

If you choose a clicker, hold the clicker in either hand. Experiment and see which hand works best for you. Ideally, you should be comfortable using either hand but start with the hand that feels most comfortable to you.

If you choose a verbal marker signal, select the word or sound you plan to use and, without your dog present, practice saying it in a happy tone of voice. See if you like the way it rolls off your tongue. I suggest choosing a word or sound which isn't part of your daily language. Timing is also an important element in dog training. Practicing your mechanical skills is important and will help you achieve good timing.

The suggested training equipment and practice exercises that follow will help you learn clean training and marker training skills.

Suggested Training Equipment

You'll use the marker signal and wearable treat bag when practicing the marking and clean training exercises in this chapter and the other equipment when practicing the exercises in the following chapters.

- A front or back clip harness for your dog—to protect the dog's esophagus and trachea should he pull.

- A marker signal—to communicate to your dog when he has performed the correct behavior.

- A wearable treat bag—provides easy access to the food you'll use to reinforce your dog. I choose to wear my treat bag behind my back, lessening the dog's interest in the food.

- A 6-foot, fixed-length leash—a safety tool and management tool.

- A 15 to 20-foot fixed-length leash—to be used after training is successful with the 6-foot leash.

- Low, medium, and high-value reinforcers—small, soft pieces of food (sized appropriately so that it's quick and easy for the dog to consume) with each value kept apart from the other (no mixing of different values and soft foods are preferable to dry biscuit-type foods).

- Water—for quenching the dog's thirst during a training session.

- Closed-toed shoes with good tread—for sure footing.

- A willingness to learn—you already have that, you're reading this book!

Marking and Treat Delivery Exercises

Now it's time to practice by yourself—alone, without your dog. If you hone your own skills before adding your dog to the training session it will set you up for success to more effectively train your

Grab your wearable treat bag, a plastic cup, and a chair. Position the chair in front of you with the chair seat facing you. Place the empty cup on the chair—think of the cup as your dog's mouth. Now you're ready for marking and treat delivery exercises.

dog. In the instructions below, the term "food hand" refers to the hand you use to deliver the treat to your dog.

Practice Exercise #1

Grab your wearable treat bag (filled with small pieces of food), a plastic cup, and a chair. Position the chair in front of you with the chair seat facing you. Place the empty cup on the chair—think of the cup as your dog's mouth.

If you're using a clicker, this will be a two-hand exercise. If you're using a verbal marker, it's a one-hand exercise. Standing with erect posture and hands at your side, use your marker signal, then reach into your treat bag with your food hand, grab one treat, place it in the cup in front of you, and return your food hand to a resting position (at your side, behind your back, or resting on your buttock).

Keeping your food hand in a neutral location prevents you from inadvertently waving the treat around in front of your dog's face and also prevents you from resting your hand in your treat bag (a big distraction for the dog).

The marker signal and the delivery of the food to the cup are two separate events, meaning the food hand doesn't move until after the marker signal: mark first, then feed. Repeat 10 times.

Practice Exercise #2

It's handy to acquire the skill of holding multiple treats in one hand for easy delivery of a reinforcer without having to reach into your treat bag.

You'll use the same tools as in the last exercise—treat bag, plastic cup, and a chair in front of you, chair seat facing you. This time you will *not* use a marker signal.

This is a one-hand exercise. Take five pieces of food out of your treat bag. Hold the five treats in your food hand and practice doling out one piece of food at a time into the cup in front of you.

If you drop a few treats, don't worry. It's a learned skill to be able to hold multiple treats in one hand and deliver one at a time. Repeat 10 times.

Practice Exercise #3

Now it's time to add the marker signal back in, followed by treat delivery to the cup. Again, this is a two-hand exercise if you're using a clicker and a one-hand exercise if using a verbal marker.

With erect posture and hands at your side, reach into your treat bag, take out five treats and hold them in your food hand. Standing with your food hand in a neutral position, use your marker signal, deliver one treat into the cup in front of you, then return your food hand to the neutral resting position (the marker signal and the delivery of the food to the cup are two separate events: mark, then feed). Repeat 10 times.

Congratulations, you successfully learned how to hold treats in your hand and mark and reinforce your dog!

[11]

Cueing:
Teaching Your Dog
the Recall Language

What is a Cue?

From the trainer's perspective (you are now your dog's trainer), a cue is a word or action we attach to a specific behavior the animal has learned in order to elicit the behavior again. It's also a signal to the dog that there's an opportunity to earn reinforcement.

In the dog-friendly and humane training I use (and hope you use, too), the word "cue" is used instead of "command." Command implies "You DO it or ELSE!"

In the world of positive training, if the dog doesn't respond to my cue, it's my job as the trainer to assess what just occurred and tweak my own actions to help the dog succeed. If the dog succeeds, the dog earns reinforcement, and reinforcement makes the behavior more likely to happen again. Just what you want!

In reality, a cue is *anything* your dog can perceive. It's also a chance to earn reinforcement. Our dogs see, hear, smell, touch, and taste, just as we do, so anything a dog is able to perceive by one of their senses can be turned into a cue.

In the companion dog world, most people use verbal cues, with hand signals coming in a close second. In canine sports and service dog work, handlers may use a number of other types of cues, including olfactory cues.

How We Confuse Our Dogs with Our Cues

All too often in training, when a dog doesn't perform the desired behavior in response to the given cue, we blame the dog.

I often hear, "He's blowing me off!" or "She's being stubborn!" But actually, the handler just didn't make it clear enough for the dog to fully understand what the person was trying to teach.

Here are a few ways we confuse our dogs when it's time to add a cue to a behavior we've taught them:

Expecting our dogs to automatically know our language. Dogs don't come with an English software package installed. We must patiently teach them our language, one cue at a time.

Not taking the time to define the goal behavior. Have in mind the specific definition of what you expect. I suggest you create a cue dictionary. Write down every cue you currently use, then define the goal behavior for each cue. Do you want a straight sit with square hips or a sidesaddle sit? A speedy down or a slow down? Defining your cues and the goal behavior for each in writing will make it clearer in your own mind about what you expect and will make it clearer for your dog.

Adding cues too early. It's important to teach your dog the behavior and make sure he can perform it reliably before adding the cue.

Using two cues simultaneously, for example, a verbal cue and a body cue (hand signal). Dogs are keen observers. They pick up on our body language before they pick up on our words. If you use a verbal cue, but also a body movement with it (such as the word "sit" and the hand signal for "sit"), I bet if you said the word and didn't use the body movement, the dog probably wouldn't understand what you meant and might not give you the behavior you expect.

Failing to reinforce the newly learned behavior enough for it to become fluent. Some dogs catch on very quickly, others more slowly, but they all can learn if we're patient and reinforce the desired behavior appropriately.

Choosing cues that look similar or sound similar. Choosing the verbal cues such as Counter and Clock for spinning in one direction then the other can be confusing for your dog because the pronounced sound of the Cs in counter and clock are similar. I suggest Spin and Twirl.

There are other reasons a dog might not respond to a cue: the dog didn't see or hear the cue; the dog didn't recognize the cue because it's too similar to another cue; the dog was distracted by the environment (another dog, a person, a squirrel); the dog felt unwell; the dog had a physical condition that prevented him from performing the behavior, or the dog felt unsafe.

So, repeat after me: "Don't blame the dog." Take a look at your training techniques and find a way to tweak the process to help your dog be successful. When your dog is successful, he earns reinforcement, and the specific behavior you worked diligently to install and put on cue works perfectly. The result is clear communication with your favorite furry friend and that's what you want for your Rocket Recall cue.

Be Clear about What You Want Your Dog to Do

It's important to know what your cues are for your dog. Yes, I bet you *think* you know, but in reality your dog may think your cues are very different than what *you* think they are.

As a professional trainer, I'm pretty good at adding cues that are clear to me and clear for the dog. But I'm human. I can make mistakes too. I've recently had a bit more time to work with Cailie. It's been a blast teaching her a few new tricks, adding humorous cues to each, and even changing a couple of cues to a few tricks I taught her some time ago. But I've seen a puzzled look on her face a few times as if she's saying, "Hey Mom, I just don't GET it. Can you be clearer?" It's evidence that it's time to clean up my cues.

How to Add a Cue

If you want to teach your dog a new behavior, you must first "show" the dog what to do and make sure the behavior is reliable before adding a cue. If you're new to modern, positive reinforcement training this may seem counterintuitive.

You'll soon learn how effective the process is in helping your dog learn cues. In the training section of this book, I'll describe how to add a cue for your dog's recall.

Our dogs know how to sit, right? They just may not know to sit when we say "Sit." For the purpose of understanding cueing, I'll use teaching sit as an example. If I'm attempting to teach a dog to sit, I would elicit the behavior by first luring, capturing, or shaping the movement.

To lure the dog into a sit, hold a piece of food in your hand, place it at the dog's nose, and move it slowly up and back over the dog's head. This causes the dog to look up, rock back a bit and as they do so, their bottom goes down. When the dog's bottom hits the floor, mark the behavior and feed him the yummy piece of food you're holding in your hand.

To capture a sit, merely wait patiently and observe the dog. When the dog happens to move into the sit position, mark and feed.

To shape a sit, consider all the tiny parts of the entire sit position (looking up, rocking back, rear end beginning to move closer to the floor), mark and reinforce each of those tiny parts toward the final behavior of sitting.

Once the dog is reliably performing the behavior (reliably means 80–90 percent of the time), you can begin to incorporate whatever cue you wish by using your desired cue *as* the dog is performing the behavior.

After the dog is successful a few times, use the cue *before* the dog performs the behavior. Example: Say "sit" (always in a happy tone of voice). Pause one second, and then lure the dog into the sit position. By pausing, you're giving the dog an opportunity to associate the sound of your verbal cue, "sit," with the behavior of sitting.

Pay close attention to your dog when you say the cue and if you see even the slightest movement that gives you an indication he's about to sit, praise him ("Good boy!") and lure him the rest of the way into the sit position, then mark and feed. By encouraging even the slightest movements, you can help increase his response to the verbal cue. With each successive repetition, slowly fade out the lure and your dog will respond to your verbal "sit" cue.

It's important to understand the cue (an antecedent, i.e., what comes before the behavior) isn't what causes the behavior to happen. The consequence of the behavior is what makes a specific behavior more likely to increase or decrease. If you like a specific behavior (the sit, down, recall, etc.) and want your dog to do it again, reinforce the heck out of it! Reinforcement drives behavior.

How to Change a Cue or Add an Additional Cue

Dogs can learn multiple cues for a single behavior. I have three different "sit" cues for Cailie: a verbal cue (an auditory cue I can use if my hands are busy), a hand signal (a visual cue I can use if I'm talking), and the sight of car keys (another visual cue I trained just for the fun of it). I must continue to use each cue periodically and reinforce it periodically if I want Cailie's response to these cues to be reliable.

If you want to change a cue, use the "new" cue, pause, then give the "known" cue, and mark and feed the correct response. Repeat several times. Next, give the "new" cue, pause a little bit longer, then give the "known" cue, then mark/feed the desired behavior. This gives the dog time to associate the new cue with the old cue.

As you continue to repeat this exercise, before long, your dog will hear the "new" cue and move into the desired behav-

photos: Bonita Ash

1) You can teach several cues for the same behavior. I taught Willow three cues for sit. Here's a hand signal. 2) which means exactly the same thing to Willow as the verbal cue. 3) and this novel cue (holding up the car keys), which I taught Willow for fun.

ior before you have a chance to give the "known" cue. You'll be excited so don't forget to mark and feed! Good job. You've just changed a cue.

Every dog learns at a different rate, just as we each do. I've seen dogs who can learn a new cue in as few as three or four repetitions. Others take longer. If you're doing a good job of minimizing your own body language, it will help your dog achieve success in a shorter amount of time.

[12]

The Four Stages
of Learning

AS YOU PROGRESS through the foundation and recall training exercises to follow, keep the four stages of learning in mind:

- **Acquisition:** You first help the dog acquire the skill of
  returning to you.

- **Fluency:** You continue to practice so the behavior becomes fluent and is occurring with regularity.

- **Generalization:** You generalize the behavior of coming
  to you by practicing in a variety of places and settings,
  always beginning in a low-distraction environment. As
  your dog makes progress, you move to slightly more
  distracting environments to practice.

- **Maintenance:** Eventually, you reach the maintenance

phase of learning, where you continue to practice recall regularly so that the behavior stays solid.

Here's how I progressed through the four stages of learning when I learned how to play the mandolin.

I first learned to play a few tunes in the privacy of my own home with no one around (acquisition). I got pretty good because I continued to practice daily and could play a lot of tunes well at home (fluency). Then I practiced playing the mandolin in a variety of places: at home with friends, at a music jam in

Following the four stages of learning resulted in a Rocket Recall for Cailie and has helped me begin to regain my skill in playing the mandolin.

public, on stage in front of an audience, then on a television show (generalization). I maintained that level of proficiency for a while by playing regularly in a variety of locations with varied distractions (maintenance).

But life got busy and I stopped practicing—no maintenance. Result? My mandolin playing isn't so great anymore. It's frustrating to realize my skill isn't what it once was, yet all I have to do is look in the mirror to see who stopped practicing.

Please know this—all is not lost if you stop practicing your Rocket Recall. Yes, your dog will lose a bit of skill, but you can help him regain it by taking training back to the beginning and moving through the systematic exercises.

I recently dusted off my mandolin. I started to practice at square one—playing scales, doing speed drills, practicing pull-offs and slides. My skill is increasing dramatically because of breaking down and practicing each individual skill before putting them all together to play a tune.

In the not-too-distant future after you finish this book and put its content into practice with your dog, you'll have a Rocket Recall and maybe, just maybe, I'll reach my former proficiency on the mandolin.

[13]

Overview of Foundation and Recall Training Exercises

HONESTY CHECK: Did you skip ahead? Reading this chapter before the rest of the book will leave you without important information designed to help you and your dog succeed. Be honest with yourself—if you skipped ahead, take a deep breath, and return to Chapter One. You'll gain valuable information that will help you navigate the practical exercises that follow.

Everything you've read so far is intended to lay groundwork for the fun task of actively training your dog. Think of the information in prior chapters as scaffolding—a structure used for supporting work.

You're about to launch into active training with your dog and the knowledge you have from the prior chapters will support you as move through training exercises.

Foundation Training Exercises for Rocket Recall

The progressive training exercises you'll be doing with your dog to bring about a successful Rocket Recall are:

The Check-In Game
- Phase One *(first indoors, off leash, then outside with dog on 6-foot leash)*
- How to Use a Long Line
- Phase Two *(your dog is on a 15-foot long line)*
- Phase Three *(your dog is off leash)*
- Problem solving for each phase

The Name Game
- Phase One *(your dog is on a 6-foot leash)*
- Phase Two *(your dog is on a 15-foot long line)*
- Phase Three *(your dog is off leash)*
- Problem solving for each phase

Using the Check-In and Name Games in Everyday Life
- Active training
- Passive training

The Rocket Recall Training Exercises
Now you're ready to train a Rocket Recall. These are the exercises:

Pick a Cue

Turn on the Cue
(in your house, with your dog on leash, then outside)
- Problem solving

The Chase Me Game
- Phase One *(your dog is on a 6-foot leash)*
- Phase Two *(your dog is on a 15-foot leash)*

- Problem solving for each phase

Round Robin Game
- Foundation Exercise for the Round Robin Game: Two People
- Problem solving
- Round Robin Game: Three People or More
- Problem solving

Practicing Recall Games in Everyday Life
- During on-leash walks about the neighborhood
- When walking with your dog on a long line in wide-open spaces that aren't safely fenced
- Anytime your dog is off leash in safely fenced areas
- When your dog is off leash and mildly distracted by something in the environment
- When your dog is playing with another dog or multiple dogs
- When your dog is engaged and focused on other people

Premack the Recall
- Eleven versions of the Premack Game

The Hide and Seek Game

The Recall and Release Game

Instructions for Training the Foundation Exercises for the Rocket Recall

Check-Ins and The Name Game

There are two important focus and attention games I play with my dogs: the Check-In Game and the Name Game. I call them games because games are fun and if you're both having fun, then training is bound to be successful.

If you decide to train your dog to do anything, your first goal is to gain your dog's attention. The Check-In and Name Game excrcises will help you accomplish this important goal. Attention is a two-way street. You'll also be learning how to pay attention to your dog.

In the following training exercises, I use the words "mark/ feed" to mean mark the goal behavior and follow with a reinforcer.

The Check-In Game

What could be better than your dog regularly offering you his attention even when you didn't ask? The Check-In Game helps your dog do just that. Whether you're enjoying on-leash or off-leash walks with your dog, he'll learn to regularly look toward you (check in) as you go about your walk. Because I've practiced these exercises regularly with Cailie, she frequently offers attention to me when we're together—no matter if she's on leash or off leash.

The Check-In Game – Phase One
(first indoors off leash, then outside with your dog on a 6-foot leash)
Goal: Your dog offers attention to you regularly without your asking
Where: Inside your house or in your yard
Training equipment: A wearable treat bag filled with treats, a marker signal (verbal or clicker), a 6-foot leash
Preparation: Practice first in a *no-distraction* environment, such as a quiet room inside your home, with your dog off leash. Wear a treat bag with treats and be ready to use your marker signal.

- Stand still and observe your dog without talking. Your goal is to say *nothing at all* while looking at your dog.

- The *instant* your dog orients toward you or looks at your face, mark/feed, and verbally praise your dog, then remove attention from the dog. Removing eye contact gives the dog permission to visually explore the environment.

- Continue to watch the dog with your peripheral vision and the moment the dog orients toward you again, mark/feed and praise.

The Check-In Game helps your dog learn to regularly offer his attention to you. Gain success with the game in the house before playing the game outside. Sit or stand still and observe your dog without talking.

The instant your dog orients toward you or looks at your face, mark his offered attention.

photos: Bonita Ash

Then reinforce him with his favorite treat.

- Repeat the game in various rooms of your home.

- Once your dog is consistently offering his attention to you indoors, practice with your dog on a 6-foot leash in slightly more distracting areas around your home (for example, on the front or back porch or patio), before moving to your front or back yard where there are lots of distractions (animal scents on the ground, passersby, etc.).

- Your goal is to help your dog always get it right. This is not about testing his limits with a newly learned skill.

Problem Solving:
- If your dog's eyes are glued to yours, toss a treat to the floor behind the dog's back. As soon as the dog finishes eating the treat, he will likely look toward you again. Then mark/feed.

- If your dog seems very distracted, instead of a full look toward you, take any approximation of looking your way. You could mark an ear turn your way or a slight turn of the head toward you.

- If at any time the exercise isn't successful, move to a lower distraction area and/or raise the value of the food used to reinforce the dog.

photos: Bonita Ash

1) In Phase One of the Check-In Game stand still and patiently observe your dog. 2) The instant he looks at you, mark his offered attention. 3) Then reinforce him with his favorite treat.

Once your dog is consistent in and around your home area on a 6-foot leash, pat yourself on the back. It's time to build upon your success.

How To Use a Long Line

In the subsequent exercises, you'll notice I suggest using a 15-foot, fixed-length leash, frequently referred to as a long line. Please do not use a retractable leash, which is not safe and is ineffective for training purposes.

If one can be in love with an inanimate object, then consider me *in love* with a long line. I use one frequently during and outside of training sessions.

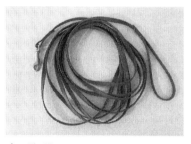

A long line is an effective management tool to prep for off-leash training. You can increase distance, yet ensure the dog stays with you. You'll use a long line as you increase distance during the recall training exercises.

photo: Lisa Waggoner

Long lines come in a variety of lengths and materials. Choose one that has a loop on one end of the line.

Long lines are made from a variety of materials: cotton, BioThane (a leather alternative), or other synthetic materials. As with a standard, 6-foot, fixed-length leash, the long line has a loop on one end for your hand and a clasp on the other end to hook to your dog's harness.

My favorite material for a long line is BioThane because it doesn't tangle easily. It's non-absorbent and doesn't get heavy from coming into contact with water, mud, or dirt. It cleans easily by wiping with a damp cloth.

In addition to using it during training sessions, I use a long line almost exclusively for leisurely walks out of doors with Cailie. It gives her the freedom to explore the world around her while keeping her safe from running off lest a pesky squirrel appear. I like to give her the choice to move toward or away from me at will—and yes, I always reinforce her for the decision to look at me or move closer to me. I live in a rural environment

photos: Bonita Ash

A long line is an effective management tool to prep for off-leash training. During training or on walks, it allows you to gather up the slack or let out the line between you and your dog as needed.

that allows me to use a long line in many places, but for walks in our downtown area, I use a 6-foot leash. A long line is less appropriate for city walks or walks in crowded areas.

Knowing how to effectively use a long line will keep you and your dog safe from injury. It's easy to get tangled around human or dog legs if you're not paying attention. Should your dog suddenly go from standing still to running with incredible velocity (squirrel!), you need a way to prevent injury.

I recommend starting with a 15-foot long line. If that's too much length for you to handle, a 10-foot line is just fine. You can progress to a 15-foot or even longer length as you gain comfort handling the extra footage. I use a 20-foot line and some trainers use up to 50-foot lines. The longer lengths are helpful when your dog's training success warrants practicing with more distance.

No matter the length of line you choose, please know you don't have to use the entire length. Your goal is to effectively gather up the slack or let out the line between you and your dog so there's no tension in the leash. The line between the two of you (no matter the distance) should stay loose—not taut.

I suggest practicing with a person first before using the long line with your dog. Find a willing friend to hold the clasp end of the leash and practice walking, then walk, trot, or run along with your friend, increasing or decreasing distance as you gather up and let out the line. You'll gain the needed long-line skill while having a few laughs along the way.

I attach the clasp end of the line to my dog's harness, then I place the loop end of the line over the thumb of my left hand, coil most of the remaining length, and put it in the same hand. As I begin walking my dog and she moves ahead of me, part of the line plays out. With my right hand, I gather up and coil any slack of the line and place it in the palm of my left hand, but stop before there is tension in the line between the dog and me. As needed, I use my right hand to gather up or let out the remaining length depending on the dog's distance from me.

When you let out the line, be sure to place any extra length of line on the ground to your side or behind you to keep legs from getting tangled in the slack. With the extra length out of harm's way, you can manage the length of the line between you and the dog by letting it drape and slide over the palm of one hand, coiling it and gently wrapping your fingers around the coil as you gather up or let out the remaining length.

If I want to move closer to Cailie, I gently pull the slack up with my right hand, quickly coil it, and place it in the palm of my left hand with my fingers loosely wrapped around the coil. If I'm not fast enough gathering up or letting out the slack, I physically move closer (to decrease) or further away (to increase) the distance between us (making sure I don't get the leash wrapped around my legs). I don't want all of the slack to be on the ground between us. The goals are to prevent tripping (or falling) and keep the dog safe.

If you happen to find yourself with part of the line wrapped around you or the dog, drop the line momentarily, step out of it, quickly pick up another part of the line, then walk yourself or your dog out of the tangled situation.

The Check-In Game – Phase Two
(with your dog on a 15-foot long line)
Goal: Your dog offers attention to you regularly without your asking
Where: In your yard and in *low-distraction* locations away from your home
Training equipment: A wearable treat bag filled with treats, a marker signal (verbal or clicker), a 15-foot leash

- Play this game first outside your home in your yard

- With your dog on the 15-foot leash, take a leisurely stroll around your house. Observe your dog, who likely has his attention elsewhere. Your goal is to say *nothing at all* while keeping your focus on your dog.

- The *instant* your dog orients toward you or looks at your face, mark/feed and verbally praise your dog. Then remove your attention and let your dog continue to do what dogs do—sniff or look around at all there is to see.

- Continue to watch with your peripheral vision and the moment the dog orients toward you again, mark/feed and praise.

- Repeat multiple times in the yard around your home until you're getting consistent success, then you can begin taking your dog to other low-distraction areas in your community (the park on a Sunday morning where there will be fewer people, etc.).

- Your goal is to help your dog always get it right. This is not about testing his limits with a newly learned skill.

Problem Solving:
- If the dog seems too distracted on the 15-foot leash, gather up some of the leash in your hand to shorten the length or return to the 6-foot leash. He'll be closer to you and will be more likely to check in with you.

- If at any time the exercise isn't successful, move to a

photos: Hannah Lozano

*1) In Phase Two of the Check-In Game you'll use a 15-foot long
line. Stand still and patiently observe your dog. 2) The instant he
looks at you, mark his offered attention and reinforce him.*

lower distraction area, and/or raise the value of your
reinforcer, or go back to where you were last successful.

The Check-In Game – Phase Three *(dog off leash)*

Once your dog is consistently achieving the goals for Phase
One and Two of the Check-In Game, it's time to practice with
your dog off leash, but always in a *safely fenced area*.

Goal: Your dog offers attention to you regularly without your asking

Where: In your yard, then safely fenced, varied locations with *your dog off leash*

Training equipment: Wearable treat bag filled with treats, marker signal (verbal or clicker)

- Go out for a leisurely stroll around your yard. Continue to observe your dog as he sniffs around and scans the environment. As always with the Check-In Game, you are to say *nothing at all* while keeping your focus on your dog.

- The *instant* your dog orients toward you or looks at your face, mark/feed and verbally praise your dog. Then remove your attention and resume your stroll.

photo: Hannah Lozano

Develop a habit of always having food on you to reinforce your dog. If you're in the yard gardening and your dog waltzes up to you to say "Hi," pay up! The more you reinforce offered check-ins, the more offered attention you'll get.

- Continue to watch with your peripheral vision and the moment your dog looks toward you again, mark/feed and praise.

- Repeat multiple times in the yard around your home until you're getting consistent success, then you can begin taking your dog to other safely fenced low-distraction areas in your community.

- Your goal is to help your dog always get it right. This is not about testing his limits with a newly learned skill.

Problem Solving:
- If at any time the exercise isn't successful, move to a lower distraction area and/or raise the value of your reinforcer. If moving doesn't help, go back to the point in training where you were last successful and practice there before proceeding again.

The Name Game

This game teaches your dog to immediately "look" toward you when the dog's name is spoken. Before I launch into the how-tos of this exercise, consider your new knowledge about how dogs learn by association (Chapter 4). You always want your dog to feel wonderful when he hears his name.

You'll be using your dog's name as his cue to look at you. His name should mean "Look at me and wait for further instruction." Saying your dog's name doesn't mean "Get out of the trash!" or "Quit chasing the cat!" or "Drop my shoe!" Please don't use your dog's name in a nasty tone of voice. If you scream at your dog when he's doing something you don't like, at best you lessen the value of his name and more likely you cement in his brain that you're an unpredictable and scary person. Always say your dog's name in a happy, loving tone of voice.

Now don't get me wrong. There are times I'm frustrated with something Cailie does. Usually, I'm frustrated with myself. For example, I've taken my eyes off her when I should have been paying attention and she got into some normal dog shenanigans (digging huge tunnels in our yard after moles). If I need to interrupt her from doing something I don't like, I use a high-pitched trill sound to interrupt her versus screaming her name. I want her to always feel awesome when she hears me speak her name.

The Name Game – Phase One
(with your dog on a 6-foot leash)
Goal: When you say your dog's name, he turns his head toward you
Where: Inside your house or in your yard on a 6-foot leash
Training equipment: A wearable treat bag filled with treats, a marker signal (verbal or clicker), a 6-foot leash

- Play this game first in a no-distraction environment, such as a quiet room inside your home, with your dog off leash.

1) *In Phase One of the Name Game stand still and wait for your dog to look away from you, then say his name in a happy tone of voice (one time and one time only). If he doesn't look at you immediately, resist the urge to repeat his name. Instead, make a kissy or squeaky noise, which will likely get his attention.*

2) *The **instant** your dog starts to turn his neck toward you, even before a full head turn, mark his response with your marker signal (verbal marker or clicker).*

photos: Hannah Lozano

3) *Then reinforce him with his favorite treat.*

- Wear a treat bag with treats and be ready to use your marker signal.

- Stand still and when your dog looks away from you, say his name in a happy tone of voice (one time and one time only). If he doesn't look at you immediately, resist the urge to repeat his name. Instead, make a kissy or squeaky noise which will likely get his attention.

- The *instant* he begins to turn his neck toward you, even before a full head turn, mark/feed and praise, then remove attention from the dog, giving him permission to look elsewhere.

- Again say his name (one time). The *instant* he orients toward you or looks at your face, mark/feed, and verbally praise your dog, then again remove attention from the dog.

- Repeat in various rooms of your home.

- Once your dog is consistently responding to his name, practice with your dog on a 6-foot leash in slightly more distracting areas around your home (on the front or back porch or patio), before moving to your front or back yard where there are lots of distractions (animal scents on the ground, passersby, etc.).

- Your goal is to help your dog always get it right. This is not about testing his limits with a newly learned skill.

Problem Solving:

- If your dog won't look away from you, toss a treat to the floor or ground behind the dog's back. As soon as the dog finishes eating the treat, say his name. When he looks toward you, mark/feed.

- If your dog is still so focused on you that he won't look away, ask a friend to join you. The added distraction of another person should be enough to cause your dog to look away.

- If you say the dog's name and he doesn't look at you, instead of repeating his name, make another sound with your voice, like the kissy noise I mentioned earlier. The odd noise should be enough to cause him to look at you, giving you the chance to mark/feed. During the early learning phase, you may need to resort to the kissy noise if he doesn't look at you when you say his name. Don't worry, he'll catch on.

- If at any time the excrcise isn't successful, move to a lower distraction area, and/or raise the value of your reinforcer, or go back to where you were last successful.

The Name Game – Phase Two
(with your dog on a 15-foot long line)
Goal: When you say your dog's name, he immediately turns his head toward you

Where: In your yard and in *low-distraction* locations away from your home

Training equipment: A wearable treat bag filled with treats, a marker signal (verbal or clicker), a 15-foot leash

- Begin this game outside your home in your yard on a 15-foot leash.

- Wear a treat bag with treats and be ready to use your marker signal.

- Take a leisurely stroll in your yard. While your dog is looking away from you (but not overly distracted by something), say his name in a happy tone of voice (one time and one time only).

- The *instant* he begins to turn his neck toward you, even before a full head turn, mark/feed and praise, then remove your attention, giving him permission to look elsewhere. Continue strolling.

- Again at a good moment, say his name (one time) in a happy tone of voice. The *instant* he orients toward you or looks at your face, mark/feed, and praise your dog, then again remove attention from the dog.

- Repeat multiple times in your yard with your dog on the 15-foot leash until you get immediate head turns when you say your dog's name.

- Once your dog is consistently responding to his name in the yard, take your training on the road and practice on leash in slightly more distracting areas in your community (the park on a Sunday morning where there will be fewer people, etc.).

- Your goal is to help your dog always get it right. This is not about testing his limits with a newly learned skill.

Problem Solving:
- If your dog is too distracted on the 15-foot long line, gather up some of the leash in your hand to shorten the length or return to the 6-foot leash. He'll be closer to you and will be more likely to respond when you say his name.

- It's much harder for your dog to look at you when he's in a new, distracting location than when he's in your house or your yard. Refrain from repeating his name. You may need to use the kissy noise again. The odd noise should be enough to cause him to look at you, giving you the chance to mark/feed.

- If at any time the exercise isn't successful, move to a lower distraction area, and/or raise the value of your reinforcer, or go back to where you were last successful.

The Name Game – Phase Three
(with your dog off leash in a fenced area)
This phase of the Name Game is similar to Phase Three of the Check-In Game. Your dog will be off leash, but in a fenced area. When your dog is consistently achieving the goals for both phases of the Name Game, he should be ready for off-leash training. Always train in a *safely fenced area*.

Goal: When you say your dog's name, he immediately turns his head toward you

Where: In your yard, then in safely-fenced, varied low-distraction locations, with your dog off leash

Training equipment: A wearable treat bag filled with treats, a marker signal (verbal or clicker)

- Go for a leisurely stroll in your yard or a safely-fenced community location. While your dog is looking away from you, say his name in a happy tone of voice.

- The *instant* he turns his neck toward you, even before a full head turn, mark/feed and praise, then remove your attention to let him check out the location. Resume your stroll.

- Again say his name (one time) in a happy tone of voice and the *instant* he orients toward you, mark/feed and praise your dog, then once again remove your attention.

- Repeat multiple times in varied locations until you get immediate head turns.

- Your goal is to help your dog always get it right. This is not about testing his limits with a newly learned skill.

Problem Solving:

- If at any time the exercise isn't successful, decrease the distance between you and your dog, move to a lower distraction area, and/or raise the value of your reinforcer. If that fails, go back to the point in training where you were last successful and practice there before moving forward again.

Using the Check-In and Name Games in Daily Life

I incorporate two different types of training with my dogs: active training and passive training.

Active training means you set aside time to train, are wearing your treat bag, and are working on a specific training exercise with your dog. "But how much time should I set aside for active training?" you ask. Generally, less is more. You can make time in your schedule for two to three five-minute active training sessions each day.

Consistency is the key ingredient to achieving training success. Always end on a positive note. If your dog has been successful with three or four repetitions in a row of your goal behavior, stop. Don't over train. Leave your dog feeling enthusiastic about your work together.

That goes for you, too. I have days when my brain is ready to train, but my body is tired. I just can't muster up the energy. We all have days when we feel like a slug. If you're not into training on any given day and can't find the enthusiasm you need, it's better to skip a day.

Passive training is any other time of the day you're *not* actively training. Your goal is to catch your dog getting it right. Consider what your dog is doing right (all those wonderful things he does that you like). Reinforce what you like, and you'll get more of what you want.

Develop a habit of always having food on you to reinforce your dog. In our house, there's rarely a time when we unload the dryer and a bit of food doesn't fall out—evidence we are ready with food in our pockets to reinforce our dogs throughout the day for behaviors we like.

If you're in the yard gardening and your dog waltzes up to you to say "Hi," pay up! The more you reinforce offered check-ins, the more offered attention you'll get. If you're sitting on the porch with your dog who is mildly distracted by something in the yard, play the Name Game. During your daily walks, practice either or both games. Remember to always reinforce your dog, preferably with food, when playing these games.

As you take training on the road and practice in new locations, always be ready to adjust your training to help your dog achieve success. Success means he'll get reinforced for checking in and responding to his name and you'll get more of what you desire!

Once you've achieved consistent success with the multiple phases of the foundation exercises, the Check-In Game and the Name Game, you're ready to begin the multiple steps of training a Rocket Recall, which are Pick a Cue, Turn on the Cue, and the Chase Me Game.

Be honest with yourself. Success means your dog is reliably checking in with you in a variety of low- to high-distraction environments and is also immediately responding to his name in the same environments. If he isn't, please continue working on those two games before moving forward.

The Rocket Recall Training Exercises

ONCE YOU'VE REALIZED SUCCESS with the Check-In Game and the Name Game, you're ready for this chapter.

Now you're ready to train a Rocket Recall. These are the exercises:

Pick a Cue

It's now time to pick the word you plan to use to call your dog.

What's the current word (the cue) you use to call your dog to you? Whatever it is, if he hasn't been reliably responding to your current recall cue at least 75 percent of the time, please pick a new cue. It's easier to condition a new cue than it is to change the emotional response to an old one.

Said another way, if you've used "come" to call your dog and he decides he'd rather go do something else—anything else—other than return to you, the word "come" doesn't have pleasant associations for him. Time to pick a new cue.

The most common cues are Come! and Here!, though I

Why not pick a fun cue? Our clients have picked Shazam! Cookie! Batman! Lottery! or Happy Hour! If your cue is a word that's fun for you to say, it'll help you be lighthearted during training. The goal is for recall training to be fun for you and fun for your dog.

highly encourage you to pick a fun cue. Our clients have picked Shazam! Cookie! Batman! Lottery! or Happy Hour! If your cue is a word that's fun for you to say, it'll help you be lighthearted during training. You want the training process to be fun for you and fun for your dog.

My own recall cue for Cailie is "Ca-Ca-Come!" which came about when she was a ten-week-old puppy (that's when I began training her recall). Because dogs respond better to higher-pitched sounds, I was in the habit of saying "Puppy, puppy, puppy" (stringing those words together rapidly in a high-pitched voice) and then running away from her to encourage her to chase me. That's my version of the puppy Chase Me Game. As she got older, I switched to "Ca-Ca-Come!" and said it in the same exciting way as I said, "Puppy, puppy, puppy!"

When you've picked the cue, it's time to help your dog understand that good stuff happens when he hears the word. You're going to Turn on the Cue.

Turn on the Cue

This exercise is designed to help your dog develop a happy feeling about the word you've chosen for your recall cue. You'll give the cue value by pairing the word with some high-value food (your dog gets to choose what's high value).

In the exercises below I'm going to pretend you've chosen the word "Shazam!" as your cue.

Turn on the Cue Exercise
(in your house with your dog on leash, then outside)
Goal: Dog develops a happy association with the sound of your recall cue because it's paired with high-value food
Where: Inside your house with your dog on leash for a week, then outside with your dog on leash
Training equipment: A wearable treat bag filled with high-value treats
Preparation: You'll practice first in a *no-distraction* environment, such as a quiet room inside your home with your dog on leash. You will *not* use a marker signal during this exercise.

- Count out 10 small pieces of food—sized appropriately so that it's quick and easy for the dog to consume (hold the pieces in one hand).

- Sit or stand with your dog in front of you. It doesn't matter what your dog is doing—he can be sitting, lying down, or standing.

- Say your recall cue, "Shazam!" and then immediately pop a treat into your dog's mouth (remember, no marker signal during this exercise). Yes, it's that simple. Say your cue, pop a piece of food in your dog's mouth.

- Repeat 9 more times.

- Practice this exercise in the house twice a day for a week.

- In the second week, practice this exercise out of doors (your back yard or porch). Repeat the above steps.

Problem Solving:
- If your dog is distracted or seems uninterested in the food, choose a higher value food and/or move to an area that's less distracting.

When I'm training this with my own dog, her eyes are bright and her body wiggles with excitement. It's as if she's thinking, "Oh my goodness, this is the most fun thing ever!"

Your dog will likely respond in the same manner at the end of the two weeks. He'll associate your chosen recall cue with the experience of eating yummy food, and you'll have created a very happy association with the cue you use to call him to come to you. You're ready to move to the Chase Me Game.

The Chase Me Game

Playing this game takes advantage of your dog's natural, genetic desire to chase. Chasing is inherently exciting for a dog, and each time the dog chases, the more reinforcing chasing becomes for him.

In some situations, such as chasing cats, you certainly want to prevent a dog from the chase while you train an alternative behavior (something the dog can do instead of chasing the cat). But in training recall, what better than to have your dog chase you? You want to build the *desire* to chase you.

Be animated and enthusiastic in your approach to this fun exercise. Find your inner cartoon character!

Ready, set, let's go!

The Chase Me Game – Phase One
(with your dog on a 6-foot leash)

Goal: Your dog *eagerly* follows you when you say your recall cue and trot three feet away

Where: Inside the house or in your yard

Training equipment: A wearable treat bag filled with high-value treats, a marker signal (verbal or clicker), a 6-foot leash

- With your dog on leash and your body facing *away* from him, look in his direction and say his name. He should immediately look at you because of all the Name Game training you've done.

- The instant he looks toward your face, say your recall cue, "Shazam!" in a very happy tone of voice and trot 3 feet *away* from him.

- As he starts to follow you, continue to verbally encourage him. When he's in movement with you, mark his behavior of following you, turn toward him, and as soon as he reaches you, put your hand on his collar and feed him a treat while telling him he's the best boy in the world.

- After you deliver the first piece of food, tell him again what a fabulous boy he is ("You're the best dog in the whole, wide world!") and continue to feed him one tiny piece of food after another for 15 to 30 seconds while you continue to exuberantly praise him. Keep in mind that 15 to 30 seconds will seem like an eternity to you, yet your dog will love lengthening the duration of the reinforcement.

- Repeat this sequence 5 or 6 times until your dog is eagerly following you.

Problem Solving:

- If you have any difficulty with this particular exercise, consider the value of your reinforcer and scan the environment to see if there's something that's distracting to your dog. You might need to raise the value of the reinforcer and/or lower the distractions in the environment. If you're unable to lower the distractions in the environment, move to another location where there are fewer distractions or return to the game where your dog was last successful.

- If your dog shies away from your hand as you reach for the collar, it's good information. Set aside time apart from this game to help your dog learn to enjoy a reach for or touch to his collar. Do this exercise: Slowly reach toward the dog's collar with one hand (coming under the dog's muzzle toward the collar) while simultaneous-

1) In Phase One of the Chase Me Game with your dog on a 6-foot leash and your body facing away from him, look in his direction and say his name.

2) The instant your dog looks toward your face, say your recall cue in a very happy tone of voice and trot 3 feet away from him. As he starts to follow you, continue to verbally encourage him. When he's in movement with you, mark his behavior of following you.

photos: Hannah Lozano

3) When your dog reaches you, reinforce him with his favorite treat and tell him he's the best dog in the whole, wide world!

ly delivering a high-value treat to the dog with the other hand. Repeat in separate training sessions as many times as it takes for your dog to feel happy about being touched and/or gently held by the collar.

Spend a week or so practicing Phase One of the Chase Me Game in and around your house, always with your dog on a 6-foot leash. When he's eagerly moving with you 100% of the time, you're ready for Phase Two. Throughout the training process don't forget to always tell him he's the best dog in the whole, wide world!

The Chase Me Game – Phase Two
(with your dog on a 15-foot long line)
Goal: Your dog *rapidly* follows you from 10 to 15 feet away when you say your recall cue and trot away
Where: In your yard or in low distraction areas outside of your home *already known* to your dog
Training Equipment: A wearable treat bag filled with high-value treats, a marker signal (verbal or clicker), a 15-foot leash

Now that your dog has gained success on a short leash, you'll transition to a 15-foot long line while continuing to play the Chase Me Game. Don't forget to find your inner cartoon character for this exercise.

- With your dog on the long line and positioned 5 to 10 feet away (you want some slack in the leash between you

In Phase Two of the Chase Me Game, your dog is on a 15-foot long line. With 10 to 15 feet between you, turn your body away from him while you look in his direction and say his name.

photos: Hannah Lozano

The instant he looks toward you, say your recall cue in a very happy tone of voice and trot or run anywhere from 5 to 15 feet away. When he reaches you, feed him a treat and deliver one tiny piece of food after another for 15 to 30 seconds while you continue to praise him.

and the dog), turn your body *away* from him while you look in his direction and say his name.

- The instant he looks toward you, say your recall cue, "Shazam!" in a very happy tone of voice and trot or run anywhere from 5 to 15 feet away.

- As he starts to follow you, continue to verbally encourage him ("Good boy!") and while he's in movement with you mark his behavior of following you, turn toward him, and the moment he reaches you, put your hand on his collar and feed him a treat while telling him he's the best boy in the world.

- After you deliver the first piece of food, continue to tell him what an amazing dog he is as you deliver one tiny piece of food after another for 15 to 30 seconds while you continue to exuberantly praise him.

- Repeat this sequence 5 or 6 times until your dog is rapidly following you.

Graduating to a 15-foot long line from a 6-foot leash is a big jump in difficulty for your dog. The distance between you and your dog makes it more challenging. If you practice in grassy areas around your home or away from your home, that's ratcheting up the difficulty even more. Put some thought into when it's appropriate to add that additional level of difficulty.

Your goal is to gradually build the distractions when you're training. Achieving success (your dog rapidly following you) is your goal.

Problem Solving:
- If for some reason your dog is slogging along during this exercise, that's beneficial information. It tells you that

something in your training plan isn't working. Go back to where your dog was successful and begin again there.

- Consider the value of your reinforcer and scan the environment to see if there's something that's distracting to your dog. You might need to raise the value of the reinforcer and/or lower the distractions in the environment.

- If you're unable to lower the distractions in the environment, move to another location where there are fewer distractions.

The Chase Me Game – Phase Three *(dog off leash)*
Goal: Your dog *rapidly* follows you when you say your recall cue and trot 5 to 10 feet away
Where: In your yard or in low distraction, *safely fenced areas* outside of your home already known to your dog
Training Equipment: Wearable treat bag filled with your dog's #1 high-value treat, marker signal (verbal or clicker), 15-foot long line available

If your dog is 100% reliable with Phase One and Two of the Chase Me game, you're ready to move to Phase Three: off-leash training. Notice that because this could be a harder job for your dog off leash, the length the dog is expected to rapidly follow is reduced to 5 to 10 feet.

- Stand near your off-leash dog.

- Turn your body *away* from him while you look in his direction, say his name, and the instant he looks at you, say your recall cue, "Shazam!" (always in a very happy tone of voice), and trot or run anywhere from 5 to 10 feet away.

- Mark his movement toward you, turn to him, and when he reaches you, again put your hand on his collar and feed him a treat (don't forget to also exuberantly praise him).

- After you deliver the first piece of food, continue to deliver one tiny piece of food after another for 15 to 30 seconds while also praising him.

- Repeat this sequence 5 to 10 times, varying the distance between you and your dog. The goal is for your dog to rapidly follow you.

Problem Solving:
- Phase Three is infinitely more challenging for a dog because he's off leash. It's a much harder job than being on leash. Dogs see their world through their nose. Think of all those amazing smells on the ground, not to mention the unusual sights and sounds in the environment. Expecting an off-leash dog outside to focus on you with those types of distractions in the environment is akin to letting a child loose in a candy store and expecting him to pay attention to you instead of all the candy. Be sure to take training at the dog's learning pace.

By now you should have an idea of how to problem solve any lack of desired response from your dog. If something isn't working, take a minute to consider what you might do to help your dog be more successful. If you change your thinking process from "My dog's blowing me off" to "My dog's having a difficult time with this exercise," it will help you be empathetic about your dog's learning process. Learning rarely occurs in a straight line.

Questions to ask yourself:
Have I moved too quickly in the training process?
Did I achieve consistent success throughout all the prior training phases?
Am I using high enough value food?
Are there too many distractions (wildlife, people, sounds, vehicles)?

Round Robin Recall Game

This version of the Round Robin Game loosely resembles a round robin tournament in the sport of tennis where each contestant meets all other contestants in turn.

In the round robin recall game, the dog will be running to one of two or more people, one person after the other, first in a pattern, and then randomly when the person calls the dog.

Foundation Exercise for the Round Robin Game – Two People

Goal: Dog eagerly runs to the person who calls and only when called

Where: Inside your house or outside with your dog on a long line or off leash in a safely fenced area

Training equipment: A wearable treat bag for each person, a marker signal (verbal or clicker), a long line available as needed

Preparation: Make sure each person's treat bag is filled with the EXACT same type of treat (otherwise, the dog will usually only return to the person with the higher-value treat). Stand or sit approximately 6 to 8 feet apart. When the dog is successful with 6 to 8 feet, gradually increase the distance between the people.

- Person A calls the dog using the chosen recall cue. When the dog is in motion to Person A, she marks the dog for coming, then delivers a treat when the dog reaches her while happily praising the dog.

- Person B calls the dog using the recall cue. When the dog is in motion to Person B, she marks the dog for coming, then delivers a treat when the dog reaches her while praising.

After a few recalls, the dog begins to pick up on the back-and-forth pattern (Person A, to Person B, to Person A again, and so forth). Before long the dog will take the treat from Person A and head off toward Person B even before that person calls. On the one hand that's great—the dog is learning this is a fun game; however, the dog only gets reinforced with the treat if the person has called the dog. What we want the dog to learn is, "When I hear the recall cue, I run to the person who called me."

In the Foundation Exercise for the Round Robin Game, the dog will be running to one of two people, one person after the other. Person A calls the dog. When the dog is in motion to Person A, she marks the dog for coming, then when the dog reaches her, she delivers a treat while praising the dog.

Person B then calls the dog. When the dog is in motion to Person B, she marks the dog for coming, then delivers a treat while praising.

photos: Hannah Lozano

The dog only gets reinforced with the treat if the person has called the dog.

Problem-solving:

- If for some reason your dog is loping along as opposed to eagerly moving during this exercise, that's great information. Not what we want, but good information nonetheless. It lets you know that something in your training plan isn't working as well as it should. Go back to where your dog was last successful and begin again there.

- Consider the value of your reinforcer and scan the environment to see if there's something that's distracting to your dog. You might need to raise the value of the reinforcer and/or lower the distractions in the environment or lessen the distance between people.

- If you're unable to lower the distractions in the environment, move to another location where there are fewer distractions.

Round Robin Game

Goal: Dog eagerly runs to the person who calls and only when called

Where: Inside your house or outside with your dog on a long line or off leash in a safely fenced area

Training equipment: A wearable treat bag for each person, a marker signal (verbal or clicker), a long line available as needed

Preparation: Every person in the game has a treat bag that is filled with the EXACT same type of treat (otherwise, the dog will usually only return to the person with the higher-value treat). Stand approximately 6 to 8 feet apart. When the dog is successful with 6 to 8 feet, gradually increase the distance between the people.

- Person A calls the dog using the chosen recall cue. When the dog is *in motion* to Person A, she marks the dog for coming, then when the dog reaches her, she delivers a treat while happily praising the dog.

- Person B calls the dog. When the dog is *in motion* to Person B, she marks the dog for coming, and when the dog reaches her, she delivers a treat while praising.

- Person C calls the dog. When the dog is *in motion* to Person C, he marks the dog for coming, and when the dog reaches him, he delivers a treat while praising. (Even though my pronoun choice for this book is "she" for the trainer, let's get the guys involved. I'm using "he" here).

- Repeat steps 1 through 3 a few times, then it's time to mix it up. Randomly choose who will call the dog. Each time the dog reaches the person who called him, that person delivers a treat and lays on the praise. As before, the dog only receives reinforcement from the person who called him.

I've yet to see a dog who didn't think this was the most amazing game in the world! What could be more fun than frolicking

photos: Hannah Lozano

The Round Robin Game loosely resembles a round robin tournament in the sport of tennis where each contestant meets all other contestants in turn. The game strengthens your dog's recall.

The dog will be running to one of two or more people, one person after the other, first in turn, and then randomly when the person calls the dog.

from person to person and eating a yummy treat? It's a fantastic way to add in some fun to your recall training.

> **Problem Solving:**
> - If the dog is hesitant to run to a specific person after he's called, she should turn the opposite direction from the dog and trot away or backward a few feet. The movement is usually enough to encourage the dog to continue moving toward that person. It's worth reiterating that if your dog displays any fear, reactivity, or aggression to people or other dogs, those behavioral challenges should be addressed first before launching into Rocket Recall training.
>
> - As always, consider distractions and the value of the reinforcers you're using. You may need to adjust one or the other or both to bring about success.

Premack the Recall

The Premack principle, known as Grandma's Law, can help you strengthen your recall training. We have the psychologist David Premack to thank for helping us learn about his theory of reinforcement, which is that a lower probability behavior can be reinforced by a higher probability behavior.

It's called Grandma's Law because it can be stated as: "Eat your veggies, then you get dessert." The lower probability behavior of a child eating vegetables can be reinforced by the higher probability behavior of eating dessert.

The Premack principle is used frequently in dog training.

Premack games are used to strengthen your dog's recall. In these photos, a lower probability behavior, running past the Jolly Ball, can reinforce a higher probability behavior, Cailie playing with the Jolly Ball.

The Jolly Ball is positioned mid-way between Cailie and Lisa.

Lisa calls Cailie, marks her behavior of coming, and is ready to reinforce her.

photos: Hannah Lozano

When Cailie reaches Lisa, she delivers one treat after another for 15 to 30 seconds.

Lisa releases Cailie to go play with The Jolly Ball.

Some people use it when teaching fetch. The dog learns that after the ball is thrown, the dog must bring the ball back and drop it (lower probability behavior) in order to have the chance to chase the ball another time (higher probability behavior).

We've used the Premack principle consistently in our Rocket Recall workshops and classes with much success. The lower probability behavior of a dog recalling to the handler while passing a person holding a bowl of chicken is reinforced when the handler accompanies the dog back to be reinforced by eating chicken from the bowl, a higher probability behavior.

The Premack Games that follow can be used after you've achieved consistent success with your dog coming to you in a variety of settings. Once you learn the concept of Premack, the ways you can incorporate Grandma's Law into your training are endless.

Premack Games

If only I could jump through these pages to sit with you and describe the fun and excitement we've had playing the Premack Games with clients and their dogs. You could feel the anticipation in the room as we described how to implement the games.

We incorporated the Premack Games at the tail end of our multi-week classes and two-day workshops. Oh my, the naysayers. I don't think we had a single client who thought their dog could succeed. Guess what? Their dog proved them wrong. Oh, ye of little faith!

That's not to say there won't be a time when your dog doesn't achieve success. That's okay. By now, you know that's merely good information and a clue for you to consider how to change things up so your dog succeeds.

The below numbered exercises are designed to be practiced in order. Play the first game and ensure success there, before moving to the next. If at any time your dog hesitates to run to you (the handler), it's time to "save the recall." Saving the recall means finding a way to encourage your dog to return to you so he earns reinforcement. Bring out your inner cartoon character. Get excited and use a high-pitched happy tone of voice. Encourage your dog to move with you by clapping your hands, patting your legs, squeaking a squeaky toy, or turning your back and running in the opposite direction. Don't be tempted to chase your dog; the better strategy is to turn and run away.

In the steps below, it's helpful to have a friend hold your dog when you call him, or you can sprinkle a few treats on the ground for your dog to enjoy while you position yourself some distance away and ready yourself to call your dog.

During each of the below scenarios, when a person is helping, the helper is standing midway and a few feet off-center from the direct path between the dog and handler.

1. The dog recalls to the handler with a low-value toy placed a few feet off the direct path, midway between the dog and handler. The dog gets a yummy treat, followed by a chance to play with the toy.

2. The dog recalls to the handler with a high-value toy placed a few feet off the direct path midway between the dog and handler. The dog gets a yummy treat, followed by a chance to play with the high-value toy.

3. The dog recalls to the handler with a low-value toy placed directly in the path, midway between the dog and handler. The dog is reinforced with a high-value treat, followed by a chance to play with the low-value toy.

4. The dog recalls to the handler with a helper standing midway and a few feet off the direct path between the

photos: Bonita Ash

Premack Game Step 2. The dog recalls to the handler with a high-value toy placed a few feet off the direct path midway between the dog and handler. The dog gets a yummy treat, followed by a chance to play with the high-value toy.

dog and handler. The dog is reinforced with a high-value treat, then led to the helper for further reinforcement with a high-value treat.

5. The dog recalls to the handler with a helper holding an empty bowl and standing midway and a few feet off the direct path between the dog and handler. The dog is

reinforced with a high-value treat, then led to the helper for further reinforcement with a high-value treat.

6. The dog recalls to the handler and passes the helper standing holding a bowl with food in it behind her back with the helper standing midway and a few feet off the direct path between the dog and handler. The dog is reinforced with a high-value treat, then led to the helper for further reinforcement with even higher-value treats.

7. The dog recalls to the handler and passes a helper standing midway and a few feet off the direct path between the dog and handler and holding a bowl with food in it at waist level. The dog is reinforced with a high-value treat, then led to the helper for further reinforcement with even higher-value treats.

8. The dog recalls to the handler and passes a helper crouching midway and a few feet off the direct path between the dog and handler, and holding a bowl with food in it at waist level. The dog is reinforced with a high-value treat, then led to the helper for further reinforcement with even higher-value treats.

9. The dog recalls to the handler and passes a helper sitting midway and a few feet off the direct path between dog and handler, and holding a bowl with food in it in her lap. The dog is reinforced with a high-value treat,

then led to the helper for further reinforcement with even higher-value treats.

10. The dog recalls to the handler and passes a helper facing forward, standing midway and a few feet off the recall path, and holding another dog on a leash, who faces away from the recall path. The dog is reinforced with a high-value treat, then led to the helper for further reinforcement with even higher-value treats (and remember to give the helper dog reinforcement too).

11. The dog recalls to the handler and passes a helper facing forward, standing midway and a few feet off the recall path, and holding another dog on a leash, who faces toward the recall path. The dog is reinforced with high-value treat, then led to the helper for further reinforcement with an even higher-value treat (and remember to give the helper dog reinforcement too!).

Note: In steps 1, 2, and 3, if your dog is overly toy motivated, you may want to enlist a helper to hold the toy (instead of placing the toy on the ground). That way, if your dog is tempted to run straight to the toy on his way to you, the helper can quickly snatch the toy so the dog doesn't have the chance to grab it.

Remember to play the first Premack Game and ensure success there, before moving to the next. If at any time your dog hesitates to run to you (the handler), it's time to "save the recall." Saving the recall means finding a way to encourage your dog to return to you so he earns reinforcement.

photos: Bonita Ash

Premack Game Step 7. The dog recalls to the handler and passes a helper standing midway and a few feet off the direct path between the dog and handler and holding a bowl with food in it at waist level. The dog is reinforced with a high-value treat, then led to the helper for further reinforcement with even higher-value treats.

photos: Bonita Ash

Premack Game Step 10. The dog recalls to the handler and passes a helper facing forward, standing midway and a few feet off the recall path, and holding another dog on a leash, who faces away from the recall path. The dog is reinforced with a high-value treat, then led to the helper for further reinforcement with even higher-value treats (and remember to give the helper dog reinforcement too).

The Hide and Seek Game

Oh, how I enjoyed this game when I was a child. If you ever played hide and seek when you were little, you likely felt the same eager anticipation I did as you searched for your hidden playmate. The search itself was exciting for me, but finally finding my hidden friend brought about uninhibited joy. I did it! I found him! That's what your dog will experience when you play hide and seek with him.

Start the game inside your house. When your dog isn't looking, quickly hide behind a door, the shower curtain, or a large piece of furniture. If your dog is too keenly focused on you to give you time to escape, have a helper hold him or scatter treats on the floor to distract him while you hide.

Make it easy at first. You want your dog to succeed. Wait for your dog to begin searching for you. If he's slow to start the search (some dogs are less motivated than others to care about their human hiding), make a slight noise, squeak a squeaky toy, or call his name, and when he finds you, celebrate with glee! Reach deep to bring out your inner cartoon character, lay on the praise, and add toys, treats, or tug as a reinforcer. You want your dog to feel triumphant in his find.

After a few repetitions of the Hide and Seek Game inside, move outside in a safely fenced area. When your dog is interested in something other than you, quickly dart behind the nearest tree or shrub (anything that hides most of your body) and wait patiently. When your dog looks away from what distracted him, he'll notice your absence and will likely begin eagerly searching to find you. Don't worry if he still needs a little help—make a slight noise or call his name if he's slow to search, then bring on the fun when he finds you.

Playing the Hide and Seek Game helps strengthen your dog's recall. When he's not looking, duck behind an object that hides most of your body and wait patiently.

photos: Hannah Lozano

When he finds you, celebrate with glee! Reach deep to bring out your inner cartoon character, lay on the praise, and add toys, treats, or tug as a reinforcer.

photo: Hannah Lozano

Lisa plays tug with Cailie. If your dog enjoys playing tug, by all means use it to reinforce him for the Hide and Seek Game or any other games described in this book.

I've played this game so frequently inside our small house that Cailie knows all my hiding places. Trust me—there aren't many. She can find me in a nanosecond, so I usually play the Hide and Seek Game outside.

During our morning walks in the pasture, when she's distracted by the scent of prey (or something else in the environment), I'll duck behind a tree, then peek out ever so slightly to watch what she does. Without fail, she'll look back (with dismay) to where I was standing as if she's thinking, "But wait, she was there just a minute ago. I must find her!" Then her fervent search begins. And yes, I do look like a cartoon character when she finds me. Sometimes I even flop on the ground and let her slather me with a million Aussie kisses to my face.

Playing the Hide and Seek Game is fun for you, builds your

dog's desire to find *you*, and it's fun for your dog. Most importantly, it's a building block to help strengthen your dog's Rocket Recall.

Recall and Release Game

The goal of this game is to help your dog understand that coming to you when called predicts that more "good stuff" will happen and doesn't always *end the fun.*

Whether it's Cailie in our pasture, your dog off leash in a safely fenced area or the dog park (not that I'm a fan of public dog parks, but you may have a safe, well-run dog park in your town), always leashing your dog after he's returned to you can cause your dog to lose interest in coming when called. Playing the Recall and Release Game will help prevent your dog's loss of interest in coming to you in similar situations.

It's time to play this game when you've reached the point in training where your off-leash dog is successfully coming to you out of doors, even if it's a short distance. When your dog returns to you after calling, reinforce him with one yummy treat and immediately release him to "go play" or "go sniff." Because he's used to sticking around for further reinforcement (those yummy treats you've been delivering for 15 to 30 seconds), you may have to encourage him to move away from you. That's okay. He'll eventually learn that "go play" or "go sniff" means *go do whatever it is you choose to do.* Then go about your walk (or gardening or whatever you were doing), let him play or sniff, call him again, and repeat the game.

Practicing Recall Games in Everyday Life

Here are some different ways to incorporate recall training into your daily life and examples of how to do it. Hint: always have food on you.

After you've trained and practiced all of the foundation and Rocket Recall exercises so that your dog is proficient with each, additional periodic practice helps your dog maintain the necessary skills.

Think back to the fourth stage of the four stages of learning. The maintenance phase is your lifelong commitment to practice in varied locations at least three times a week for life.

"Do I really have to do that?" you ask?

Only if you want your recall to stay strong. I bet you do.

My barometer for gauging Cailie's success with a specific training exercise is her *automatic* response to the given cue. My training goal is for her to *respond without having to think* about what she should do. Not having to think about it means she gives me an *immediate* response to any of the cues associated with the foundation exercises or recall game exercises. The moment I say the cue, she begins responding.

If you drive a vehicle, I bet you have an *automatic* response to seeing brake lights on the car in front of you.

Think of brake lights as a cue. The sight of brake lights causes you to take your right foot off the accelerator, move that foot slightly to the left, and press on the brake pedal, which prevents you from running into the stopping car in front of you. You've performed this exercise so frequently that it's not necessary to logically think through the chain of three behaviors necessary to *stop the car*.

That's what you want for your dog. While there's no rocket-like speed with our fourteen-year-old boy, Cody, he still has an automatic response to Brad's recall cue, now a loud hand clap (one of the only sounds he still appears to hear). He can be head-down sniffing something in the pasture and when Brad calls, it's almost as if his body begins moving toward Brad before his nose even leaves the scent—evidence he doesn't have to think about what to do. It's automatic.

[16]

Everyday Life Training Opportunities

THERE ARE MYRIAD WAYS to easily add recall training into your everyday life. Take advantage of the suggestions below to strengthen your dog's recall once or twice a day (or more).

During on-leash walks about the neighborhood.
As you're briskly walking together in one direction, say your dog's name in a happy tone of voice, and as he looks at you, slowly trot away in the opposite direction. Mark/feed when he follows you and praise.

When your dog is sniffing the ground, wait for him to *begin to disengage* from the scent, say his name, and when he looks your way, say your recall cue and trot in the opposite direction. Mark/feed when he follows and don't forget to lay on the praise.

Say his name when he's looking at something on the other side of the road. When he looks back, mark/feed and praise.

Any time your dog looks at you during the walk, mark/feed and praise—he just checked in with you!

When walking with your dog on a long line *(15- to 20-foot long line)* **in wide-open spaces that aren't safely fenced.**
You can use the same procedure as on-leash walks, only you'll have much more distance between you and the dog when you're using a long line. I never fail to practice each one of the recall games when I'm walking with Cailie on a long line in a new location. Each successful check-in, name response, or recall (no matter the distance) helps bring about further success.

Anytime your dog is off leash in a safely fenced area.
It's important for your dog to have off-leash time to stretch his legs and get some physical exercise before you begin off-leash recall training in your everyday life.

I'm forever grateful that we have seven safely fenced acres around our home. As we head out for a morning walk, Cailie's always off leash (unless we plan to walk outside the gate and through the ten acres of wooded land outside the fence—then I use a long line). I vary the games and never fail to reinforce her in some manner (sometimes food, sometimes praise, sometimes both) for an offered check-in, response to her name, or a blazing recall across the pasture.

You may have to search for a safely fenced area where you can practice off leash. It doesn't have to be a wide, open space— you can use a friend's fenced back yard, a softball field, or a tennis or pickleball court (with permission, of course). You can also checkout Sniffspot.com, a large community of safe private spaces for dogs to play (rental prices vary, but are usually quite low). What's important is that you find new and different, safely fenced areas to practice the recall games. This helps your dog gain success in different environments with different smells and distractions.

When your dog is off leash and *mildly* distracted by something in the environment *(another person, another dog, a sound, etc.)*.
I always try to anticipate my dog's response before I make the decision of which game to play and how far away I'll be from my dog. My goal is her success with my chosen plan. Practice any one of the games (Check-In, Name Game, Turn on the Cue, or the Chase Me Game). Vary the games throughout the time you're enjoying together.

When your dog is playing with another dog or multiple dogs.
Here's an early training example of my calling Cailie during multi-dog, off-leash playgroups. I waited until Cailie played for five or ten minutes and was beginning to tire from playing with the other dogs. As she began to disengage from the group, I positioned myself only a few feet away from her (my body facing away from her), I called her name and as she immediately looked at me, I said my recall cue (in a very happy tone of voice), then ran away from her. When she began to follow, I praised her as if she was the best dog in the whole wide world (she is, of course), I marked the behavior (following me) with a verbal "Yes!" and then I reinforced her with her favorite treats, feeding one right after the other. Practicing this way, over time, now allows me to call her away from other dogs when she's still engaged in play. Pretty amazing!

When your dog is engaged and focused on other people.
If your dog is a social butterfly, this can be challenging—it just depends on how exciting other people are to your dog. Cailie is over the moon for any person, new or known. Coming away from a person or a dog is a really hard job for her, so I always pay her well. Your dog can be on leash or off leash as you practice when he's focused on another person. What's most important is that you have an idea of how hard a job it will be for your dog to 1) check in with you, 2) respond to his name, or 3) disengage with the person when you call him to come using your recall cue. An intense focus or engagement on the other person means you should lessen the distance between you and that individual.

During any of the above situations, please consider the success you've previously achieved with training. Your goal is to call your dog to you only when you're pretty darn certain he'll come. Set him up to get it right by not asking for too much. Remember reinforcement drives behavior. It's the reinforcement for a successful repetition of the recall game that makes it more likely to achieve the result you want—your dog coming to you when you call.

[17]

Climbing Over Speed Bumps During Training

OH HOW I WISH any type of learning—for humans or for dogs—occurred in a straight line. If that were true, I'd be the most proficient mandolin player in the whole wide world. Yet learning never occurs in a straight line.

Even when you're exactly following the recall training steps and introducing distance and distractions at a gradual pace to ensure your dog achieves success with each step before moving to the next, you're bound to hit some training speed bumps along the way.

Something just won't work out as you intended. That's okay. It's not only okay, it's expected—there's individuality in learning. Your individuality in reading, understanding, and implementing the recall training exercises, individuality in the way you apply the techniques, individuality in your dog's ability to grasp the concept, and individuality in how frequently you practice.

My mandolin teacher always says, "Don't practice your mistakes." That's good advice to apply to dog training, too. If something doesn't work during one repetition of a particular training exercise, consider it good information. Before the next repetition of the exercise, ask yourself a few questions and consider how you might change one or more of the following:

- The antecedents (all those things that are in the environment before you start training).

- Your body language (which can be confusing or distracting to the dog).

- How much you're asking of the dog. Are you training in an area where the distractions are too overwhelming for him?

- The appropriate value of reinforcer for the task at hand (remember the reinforcement hierarchy in Chapter 9).

- Health and wellness—no one can learn when they're not feeling well.

All of the components should blend together in just the right combination to set your dog up for success...to get it right.

Video your training sessions. Everyone has a smartphone these days. Buy yourself an inexpensive, extendable tripod to hold your phone. I use a Fugetek tripod I found online for only $15. It's advertised as a selfie stick and tripod. It's lightweight and portable, has non-skid feet, and comes with a Bluetooth remote. Because it's extendable, I can vary the height to ensure I get the view I need for a particular training exercise.

If you haven't videoed yourself training, when you play back the video you're going to be tempted to pick apart everything you did that wasn't exactly perfect. That's normal. Do you remember the first time you ever recorded your voice? I don't know about you, but I was aghast at the way I sounded...why, that wasn't MY voice I was listening to! I was very critical of how I sounded.

It's rather the same way watching yourself in a video. Yes, you may see a few things you could do differently to make the training exercise more effective—that's why you video the session. However, I'd bet a hundred dollars that you did a lot of things right.

Most people tend to overlook what they did right and focus on what they did wrong. Please be kind to yourself and change your thinking. What you perceive as wrong is merely information that will help you. If you see three things you can improve upon, I want you to replay the video to find six things you did just right.

Always keep this in mind: if you notice needed areas of improvement, that's information to help you tweak your training plan to achieve success.

[18]

Common Training Mistakes

NOW THAT YOU UNDERSTAND the systematic training steps for Rocket Recall, here are a few common training mistakes that can occur. If any of these have occurred at your home, don't worry—refer back to the individual foundation and training exercises and you have a path forward to success.

Not Training

Not training is definitely a training mistake. Recall is a learned behavior, just like anything else you wish to teach your dog. You must train your dog to respond to your recall cue (the word you use to call your dog to you).

Recall isn't hard to teach and it's not hard to practice regularly, but you must train the foundation behaviors first. Once those are reliable, you'll begin the step-by-step systematic process of teaching your dog to enthusiastically return to you using the Rocket Recall training exercises.

Wouldn't it be nice if dogs came with an English software

package installed? Ah, but they do not. Dogs don't understand our spoken language. If we merely say "come!" and expect them to comply by understanding that English word, disappointment usually follows.

It's up to each one of us to teach a dog the recall behavior and then add the verbal cue so the dog understands what the cue means. Once the cue is added, you continue to practice the skill so your dog learns the behavior of coming to you in varied locations with varied distractions.

Doing the Initial Training But Not Practicing

Once you've trained your dog to reliably return to you, continued practice is necessary to achieve consistent success in the future. Keep the four stages of learning in mind:

- **Acquisition:** You first help the dog acquire the skill of returning to you.

- **Fluency:** You continue to practice so that the behavior is fluent and is occurring with regularity.

- **Generalization:** You generalize the behavior of coming to you by practicing in a variety of places and settings, always beginning in a low-distraction environment. As your dog makes progress, you move to slightly more distracting environments to practice.

- **Maintenance:** Eventually you reach the maintenance phase of learning, where you continue to practice recall regularly so that the behavior stays solid.

Remember, it's the consistent practice of a newly learned skill that creates strength in a behavior.

Failing to Reinforce the Dog

Here's a common scenario: People teach their dog to return to them when they say "come"—but fail to continue practicing. They use the word very casually while taking the formerly much sought-after behavior for granted and failing to acknowledge, much less reinforce the dog for returning. Reinforcement is what drives behavior.

For example, imagine that you say the word "come" to call your dog when he's outside enjoying himself. He returns to you the first time you call because you're nice to him and you feed him; there's a bit of reinforcement history between the two of you. But then you bring him inside the house, you pick up your car keys, and you go to work.

From your dog's perspective, you've just taken the "good stuff" away (the outdoors with all those awesome smells) and ignored him (by locking him inside and going to work). In dog training (and human learning) taking the good stuff away constitutes punishment, and punishment makes the behavior of coming to you less likely.

All Is Not Lost

Again, please understand that if any of these common training mistakes has occurred or inadvertently occurs in life with your dog at some point in time, all is not lost. Review the training methodologies in this book, return to where your dog was last successful, and begin recall training with a refreshed knowledge of how to proceed.

[19]

Considerations for Training Around Prey

PREY IS THE ULTIMATE DISTRACTION for many dogs, if not most. Dogs are predators with a genetic predisposition to be interested in prey. Whether it's the smell, sight, sound, or movement of the prey, most dogs are distracted to some degree when prey or the scent of prey is present in their environment.

Please know this—no matter how much time and practice you put into teaching and training your dog to have a solid, long-distance, off-leash recall, there's always a chance your dog will choose prey over your recall cue. That's why my own behavior has changed over the last decade. I used to frequently enjoy hiking with my dogs off leash. There's such a thing as deadly trust.

Can I be certain Cailie will always return to me—even in the presence of prey? No. She can easily cover seven acres in the blink of an eye. Even though we live on seventeen acres in rural North Carolina, only part of that is fenced. If we're outside the fenced area and prey appeared, no doubt she'd become aroused—her predatory instinct could kick in, and if she decided to chase, I suspect with her blazing speed she could easily run two miles to the main, two-lane road. That's a risk I no longer wish to take.

Dogs in the wild who can find, catch, kill, and consume prey live to see another day. Catching and consuming aren't needed in today's world when canine companions have the luxury of being served their meals by a capable human, but a dog's genetics still come into play.

Over the last hundred years or so, selective breeding for specific qualities (lap-sitting vs. herding for example) has lowered the strength of predatory behavior in some domestic dogs. Even within the same breed, certain dogs will have stronger behavioral responses to prey.

Cailie is the fifth Australian Shepherd dog we've had the pleasure of adding to our home. She's by far the dog with the strongest predatory behavior. Even as a young puppy I noticed her orienting to the scent of prey much more than any of our other puppies. She displays the entire basic predatory motor pattern sequence which is: orient > eye > stalk > chase > grab-bite > kill-bite > dissect > consume.

Ray and Lorna Coppinger's book *Dogs: A New Understanding of Canine Origin, Behavior and Evolution*, discusses the variety of slightly different motor patterns for specific breeds. If you want to learn more about the behavior and evolution of dogs, including predatory behavior, it's a good read.

In our fenced acreage, we usually walk with our dogs off leash. Believe me, the first time I saw Cailie chase, catch, bite, kill, and consume a rabbit I was horrified. A bunny—she ate a bunny! The reality is that my canine daughter is, after all, a dog. She did what came naturally to her.

Understanding your dog's genetic predisposition to be interested in prey will help you design effective management strategies for working in and around such a high-level distraction. Your understanding will aid you when planning a recall training session. In fact, anytime you're training out of doors—no matter the skill you're working on with your dog—it's important to consider your dog's behavior around prey. That's why it's necessary to begin all training indoors when teaching your dog a new skill, and that includes recall training. Once your dog is successful indoors, then, and only then, should you train outside.

So what to do about prey during recall training? Remember my suggestion to always create an environment that sets your dog up for success. You will create a management strategy and training plan to practice your dog's newly-learned, indoor, recall skill around prey. What's difficult about this phase of training is that it's hard to control the prey.

Oh, if I could only banish from our property the feathered and furry creatures that cause Cailie to lose her thinking brain. The prey I have to contend with—perhaps I should say compete with—during training outside our home are most often birds, chipmunks, squirrels, rabbits, and deer. We also have opossums and raccoons.

Birds are not much of an issue unless one happens to hit a window in mid-flight and falls to the ground—the sound of the impact or the movement of the bird falling will cause her to run toward the bird.

I don't have to worry about planning training sessions for Cailie with opossums and raccoons nearby because they're nocturnal. However, I do have to be extremely vigilant with management after dark because of those two animals. Even though we bring the bird feeders in at night, opossums and raccoons frequently roam our yard after dark scarfing up leftover birdseed that spilled during the day while birds enjoyed the seed. Even if we didn't have feeders, opossums and raccoons roam our rural area with regularity and would likely enter our yard.

Bad experience creates good judgment. I've had the unfortunate experience of having to break up a dog and raccoon fight—a raccoon and Cailie. Another time she snatched an opossum in her mouth as it was roaming around our back porch. Nope, she didn't want to let go of it. Now before I walk outside at night, I take a quick walk around our home with a flashlight to ensure no prey is inside the fence (management—preventing access to prey).

Thankfully it was an incredibly strong reinforcement history with her Jolly Ball that brought about success in breaking up the raccoon fight and causing her to drop the opossum. The opossum was playing dead, but a non-moving animal (or even a dead one) is highly distracting for many dogs. The Jolly Ball has always been one of her favorite toys. Because she's a herding dog, she loves to chase. The opportunity to chase the ball is highly reinforcing by itself. I've also used chasing the ball to reinforce her distance recalls when deer are in sight. It's useful during the Premack exercises too. It was priceless during the opossum encounter (and potentially life-saving). Say hallelujah to the Jolly Ball!

A standard leash or a long line is your management strategy when training around prey. Even with your dog on leash to prevent him from being reinforced by running off and chasing prey, learning when to interrupt your dog when he is focused on prey is important.

Think again about the predatory motor pattern orient > eye > stalk > chase > grab-bite > kill-bite > dissect > consume. The sooner you can interrupt your dog in the sequence the better chance you have of gaining your dog's attention.

I'm able to interrupt Cailie at the ORIENT, EYE, and STALK phase of the sequence and at the beginning of the CHASE phase (even when deer are running away from her), but only because I have frequent chances to practice her recall in the presence of deer. Most dogs are highly aroused when chasing prey—meaning that their focus will most certainly be on the prey animal and not you, unless you've methodically trained and practiced the exercises I suggest.

The foundation and recall training exercises you've learned can and should be used when training your dog around prey. Be systematic in your approach to using the training exercises, realizing prey is the ultimate distraction. Just because you have a rock-solid, out-of-doors, long-distance recall when no deer are present doesn't mean you'll have success recalling your dog from deer—unless you train in the presence of deer. Because it's hard to control the prey, you may choose to always leash your dog in areas where prey is prevalent.

I've trained Cailie to recall from deer standing, walking slowly, and running in our pasture. Admittedly, I'm lucky because I can control her access to deer, even if she's off leash, because of the fenced acreage around our home and pasture.

The deer jump the fence in any number of places in the back five acres, but never venture close to the house and have never jumped over the fence surrounding our house. This allows me to use the foundation and recall training exercises in the presence of deer.

After moving through each of the foundation training and recall exercises with Cailie outside and on leash, followed by training using a long line, and finally progressing to off-leash recall training, she has a solid long-distance recall from anywhere within our seven acres of fenced pasture.

But even with such success, when I decided to train her in the presence of deer, I started from scratch—meaning I went back to square one and used a 6-foot leash and practiced The Name Game, Check-In Game, and all phases of the Chase Me Game as frequently as possible when deer happened to be out in the pasture. If only I could text the deer and say, "Hey, can you come provide a bit of distraction so I can work on recall today?" I was, and continue to be, limited in my ability to implement training in the presence of deer. This will be true for most of you who live in the midst of wildlife.

After Cailie gained success with training around deer while on a 6-foot leash, I used the long line and achieved further success before moving to off-leash training in the presence of deer.

But deer are not the strongest distraction for Cailie. I often use her Jolly Ball (a high-value reinforcer) to reinforce her coming to me in the presence of deer—other times I can use different medium or high-value reinforcers (chosen depending on the distance between her and the deer).

Rabbits are our nemesis. If only I could control the bunnies! Alas, I cannot, but I try. During the early breeding season in spring, when cottontail rabbits are most prevalent, we close our gates to the back pasture—a management strategy so that Cailie doesn't have access to our pasture area where rabbits are prone to make their dens. But that doesn't keep them from hopping through the fence into the yard around our house.

Remember that Cailie chased, took down, and ate a rabbit— that's huge reinforcement that adds to the distraction power of bunnies. Even rabbit scent on the ground causes her to lose focus on all else.

I'm only beginning to train her to focus on me in the presence of fresh rabbit scent. I bought rabbit scent online. An itsy, bitsy, tiny bit of the liquid (what might fit on a pinhead) caused her to immediately lose focus on me. I couldn't smell it, but there was no doubt about the fact she could by the speed with which her eyes dilated as if she was thinking, "OMG, it's a bunny!"

I'll begin the foundation and recall exercises as written in this book with Cailie on a 6-foot leash and the rabbit scent present in the environment. The closer she is to the scent, the more challenging it will be for her. I know I need to begin with the scent positioned a sufficient distance away from our training location. I'm sure I'll learn more about her predatory behavior and the need for selective reinforcers to pay her for focusing on me or returning to me when I call.

And I'll use the Premack principle too. As I gain progress with her skill of returning to me with the rabbit scent present, I'll call her to me and then give her the opportunity to "go sniff" the rabbit scent.

If you remember back to the Reinforcers, Distance, and Distractions chapter, a distraction can also be a reinforcer. While it's not possible to use all distractions as reinforcers, in Cailie's case, I can use the rabbit scent I purchased to reinforce her for focus on me when a natural rabbit scent is present. I also purchased a rabbit pelt to make into a tug toy for just that purpose—reinforcement. It pained me greatly to think a rabbit lost its life for me to have the pelt. I hope to save a few rabbits from a premature demise by training Cailie to focus on me versus a rabbit.

[20]

A Quick Reference Guide to Recall

THE TWELVE RULES BELOW are designed as a quick reference guide to help you remember some of the most important components to achieving a Rocket Recall.

The 12 Rules of Rocket Recall

What is a Rocket Recall? It's that glorious moment when anytime and anywhere you say "Come!" your dog immediately and enthusiastically turns on a dime and bounds rapidly to you.

1. Train it! Practice it!
   - Recall is a learned behavior—just like anything else you teach your dog.
   - Practice indoors first so the behavior is solid before moving out of doors.
   - Indoor/off-leash recall is like a High School Diploma: not too difficult to get.

- Outdoor/off-leash recall is like a PhD: you must train for it.
- Make it FUN! If it's fun for you, it'll be fun for your dog!

2. **Use the highest-value reinforcers for recall practice.**
   - Reinforcement makes behavior stronger—always reinforce your dog.
   - The reinforcer must be something your dog will do "backflips" over.
   - Reinforcers most dogs love: hot dogs, cheese, Vienna sausage, baked chicken, steak, smoked salmon. Experiment. Use what *your dog* loves.
   - When your dog comes to you, reinforce with one small bit of food after another for 15 to 30 seconds while praising your dog.

3. **Reinforce ALL check-ins during other times of the day.**
   - A "check-in" is anytime your dog chooses to visit you on his or her own accord.
   - When your dog trots over to say "Hi" to you, praise and reinforce with a piece of yummy food; smile, be joyful!
   - Reinforcing check-ins will help your dog stay closer and check in more frequently.

4. **Never call a dog for anything the dog doesn't like.**
   - If you call your dog to come and then do something to him he doesn't like, such as a bath, nail trims, or administering medications, this is likely punishing.
   - Punishment decreases behavior—not what you want with recall.
   - If it's time for you to do something to your dog he doesn't like, just go get your dog—don't use your recall cue.

5. **If you don't think your dog will come, don't waste the cue.**
   - If your dog is chasing a squirrel or playing with another dog and his recall isn't strong, using the cue will likely be ineffective anyway.
   - You want your dog to be successful!
   - Success means your dog earns reinforcement (something the dog loves).
   - Reinforcement increases the likelihood the behavior will happen again.

6. **If you make a mistake on #5 by using the cue and the dog doesn't respond, "save" the recall.**
   - "Saving the recall" means to find a way to encourage your dog to return to you so he earns reinforcement.
   - Encourage your dog to move with you by clapping your hands, patting your legs, squeaking a squeaky toy, turning your back, and running away.

- Never chase your dog; the better strategy is to turn and run away.

7. **Say the cue only once—never repeat the cue.**
   - Repeating the cue over and over creates "learned irrelevance." Dogs learn to ignore things that have no meaning.
   - If you say your cue and the dog doesn't immediately respond, find your inner cartoon character!
   - Make yourself interesting with a high voice, clapping, squatting, etc.

8. **Never punish your dog if your dog doesn't "come" when called.**
   - Dogs make decisions based on what's safe and what's not based on consequences.
   - If you've punished your dog, he won't come to you or will be fearful of returning to the "scary human being."
   - Even if your dog initially ran the other way when you called, reinforce and exuberantly praise your dog upon his return.

9. **Always give the dog a HUGE pay-off.**
   - Always use high-value foods as reinforcers or if your dog loves to tug, then play tug.
   - During the training process, reinforce your dog with

food or tug for 15 to 30 seconds *each and every time he comes to you.*

- Once you're in the maintenance phase of recall training, continue to reinforce your dog every time your dog comes.
- Vary the reinforcers: food, a game of Chase Me (you run away, your dog follows), a toy, a game of tug, fetch, etc.

10. **Maintain it after you train it.**
- The trainer should commit to practicing in varied locations at least three times a week for life.
- Remember the four stages of learning:
    - Acquisition (learning to do the behavior)
    - Fluency (getting really good at it so that it's automatic)
    - Generalization (learning to do it anywhere and everywhere)
    - Maintenance (lifelong commitment to reinforce so the behavior is strong)

11. **Play the Hide and Seek Game with your dog. It's fun for you, builds the desire in your dog to find you, and it's FUN for both of you!**
- Play indoors or outdoors in a safely fenced area.
- When your dog isn't looking, quickly hide behind a door, shower curtain, or tree outside (make it easy at first; you want the dog to succeed).

- Wait for your dog to begin searching for you.
- Make a slight noise or call his name if he's slow to start the search.
- Celebrate with glee when he finds you—throw a party!
- Lots of verbal praise, cartoon character antics, toys, or treats.

12. Recall and Release

- When your dog successfully returns to you, reinforce and immediately release your dog to "go play" so the recall doesn't always *end the fun*.

[21]

Conclusion

THERE'S INCREDIBLE PEACE OF MIND that comes with knowing your dog will reliably return to you anywhere and anytime when you call. It will help you enjoy more fun, off-leash activities, and it can also save your dog's life.

Thank you for sticking with me through the early explanatory chapters of this book; each was designed to give you information about why training works and what to do if it doesn't, resulting in understanding.

Understanding is a key component of any trainer's toolkit—equally important, if not more, than tangible tools. Remember that learning doesn't occur in a straight line. You're bound to experience peaks and valleys in your learning and your dog's learning. That's why I've given you the tools to problem solve any training speed bumps you encounter along the way.

If only I could teleport myself to your home and hover by your side to witness the fun I anticipate you and your dog will experience as you work through the foundation and Rocket Recall exercises together. I've endeavored to make recall training enjoyable for both you and your dog. My goals are always safety first, followed by fun and, of course, effective training.

Once you achieve the coveted Rocket Recall, I'd love to hear about your success! Feel free to share your training videos or comments about your progress with me by email or on the Cold Nose College Facebook page. Your success is my goal. Hearing about your progress is reinforcing and motivates me to continue sharing humane, modern training techniques with the public.

So get up, get going, start training, and you'll be on your way to getting that sought-after Rocket Recall from your dog, every time.

Happy Training!

Glossary

ABCs—Three elements (antecedent, behavior, consequence) used to analyze behavior

acquisition—The process of acquiring a skill

active training—Training that is set up with advance preparation and a plan

alternative behavior—A behavior the dog can do instead of performing an unwanted behavior

antecedents—The conditions present prior to a behavior; contributing factors to a dog's behavior

auditory cue—The signal or sound a dog hears that causes the dog to perform a trained or untrained behavior

automatic response—The response to a stimulus that occurs without the dog having to think

aversives—Anything a dog finds distasteful, uncomfortable, or painful

behavior—The way a person or animal acts in response to a certain stimulus

BioThane—A brand name of a coated webbing product used as a leather alternative

body cue (or signal)—A hand or other body signal a dog perceives as an indicator to perform a behavior

check-in—The act of a dog voluntarily offering attention without being cued

classical conditioning—Learning by association; the process by which an animal learns to associate events over which it has no control

clean training—How a handler minimizes extraneous movement of their entire body (or parts of the body) during a training session

clicker—A small plastic device with metal inside used to mark a dog's behavior and which bridges the gap between the time the behavior happens and the delivery of the reinforcer

command—A cue or signal for an animal to perform a behavior (a term not used in positive reinforcement dog training because it implies "do it or else")

conditioned fear response—A state of anxiety or fear that occurs because the dog was exposed to a stimulus that was formerly neutral but has been paired enough times with something scary

conditioned stimulus—A previously neutral stimulus that because of pairing with an unconditioned stimulus eventually produces a conditioned (learned) response

consequence—The action or environmental change that follows a behavior; what happens after a behavior that makes it more or less likely for the behavior to happen again

crossover dog—A dog previously trained using aversive techniques whose handler learned about humane training and crossed over to using positive reinforcement training

cue—A signal a dog perceives as an indicator to perform a behavior

discriminative stimulus—The cue or stimulus present when the behavior a dog displays is reinforced; said another way, a stimulus in the presence of which a response will be reinforced

distance—How far away you are from a dog when training the dog to perform a behavior; one component of the Three Ds

distraction—Anything present in the training environment that causes a dog to focus on something other than the handler or the requested behavior; one component of the Three Ds

duration—The length of time a dog holds a position or performs a behavior; one component of the Three Ds

fluency—The process of performing a behavior easily and accurately

food hand—The hand used to deliver a reinforcer to the dog

force-free dog training—A method of training that strives to always keep the dog comfortable during the learning process, teaching the dog without pain, coercion, threats, or force

four stages of learning—The four components (acquisition, fluency, generalization, and maintenance) involved when a dog or person is learning something new

generalization—Practicing a newly learned behavior in a variety of places and settings so the dog gains skill and can reliably perform the behavior

genetic predisposition—An increased chance of a dog displaying a particular behavior based on the dog's genetic background

Grandma's Law—A lay term for the Premack Principle; eat your veggies and then you'll get dessert; a way of saying a less probable behavior (eating vegetables) can be reinforced with a higher probable behavior (eating dessert)

handler—The person who is training the dog

hand signal—A signal made with a hand (or hands) that a dog perceives as an indicator to perform a behavior

humane training—A method of training that strives to always keep the dog comfortable during the learning process, teaching the dog without pain, coercion, threats or force

individuality in learning—The process by which a dog or a person processes information and increases knowledge; the process is different for each dog and each human

inner cartoon character—The part of yourself that is capable of acting ridiculously silly and jolly, doing such things as jumping up while clapping your hands, patting your legs, squeaking a squeaky toy, or turning your back and running in the opposite direction from a dog to encourage the dog to excitedly return to you

Jolly Ball—A durable dog ball made by Jolly Pets that a dog can push with his nose or paw

The Law of Effect—Edward Thorndike's theory that responses that produce a satisfying effect in a particular situation become more likely to occur again in that situation, and responses that produce a discomforting effect become less likely to occur again in that situation

learned irrelevance—A type of selective learning that occurs when a dog has learned that a stimulus (such as a cue) that is repeated over some time comes to have no meaning (meaning nothing important happens for the dog)

long line—A ten to twenty-foot (or longer) leash that can be made from a variety of materials

maintenance—The act of continuing to practice and reinforce a trained behavior a dog has learned

management—Manipulating a dog's environment to prevent

the dog from practicing an unwanted behavior while training an alternative behavior

management strategy—creating a plan to arrange an environment that prevents a dog from practicing an unwanted behavior

marker—A sound or other signal that marks a desired behavior of the dog and becomes a communication tool to help them understand that reinforcement will occur

marker signal—A sound or other signal that marks a desired behavior of the dog and becomes a communication tool to help him understand what will earn him reinforcement

negative punishment—A process of operant conditioning where something desirable is taken away in an attempt to decrease a behavior

negative reinforcement—A process of operant conditioning where something undesirable is taken away in an attempt to increase a behavior

olfactory cue—A chemical signal sensed through a dog's nose that becomes an indicator to perform a behavior

olfactory distraction—A smell in the environment that causes a dog to focus on the smell instead of the handler

operant conditioning—A process by which a dog (or person) makes an association between a particular behavior and a consequence.

palatal click—The sound made when the tip of a human tongue is touched to the roof of one's mouth and released quickly (the sound resembles a pop)

passive training—Any time outside of a formal training session when a dog receives reinforcement for a behavior the handler likes

pay your dog—Give your dog a reinforcer

positive punishment— A process of operant conditioning where something is added in an attempt to decrease a behavior

positive reinforcement—A process of operant conditioning where something is added in an attempt to increase a behavior

predator—An animal that lives by killing and consuming other animals

Premack principle—A theory of reinforcement, developed by David Premack, which states that a lower probability behavior can be reinforced by a higher probability behavior

prey—An animal that is sought, captured, and eaten by a dog or other animal

primary reinforcer—Something that is biologically important to all dogs, such as water, food, safety, and sleep

punishment—A consequence that causes a behavior to decrease

punishment callus—A term used to describe the tolerance an animal develops from repeated exposure to punishing training techniques

random reinforcement—Also referred to as intermittent reinforcement; a schedule of reinforcement where the dog or other animal receives a reinforcer at irregular intervals

recall—The act of dog returning to the handler when called

reinforcement—A consequence that causes a behavior to increase

reinforcement hierarchy—A list of reinforcers and distractions ranked from lowest to highest value

reinforcer—Something of value given to an animal to strengthen a behavior

Rocket Recall—The act of a dog immediately and enthusiastically returning to the handler when called

save the recall—A process used when a dog hesitates to respond to the recall cue; to animatedly encourage a dog to return to you so that he earns reinforcement

secondary reinforcer—Something a dog has learned to value because of the pairing with a primary reinforcer

speed bumps—Inevitable challenges that pop up during the process of learning something new

stimulus—Anything that triggers a behavioral or physical change

systematic—Methodical in procedure or plan

taking training on the road—Moving to new locations to practice a skill after a dog has successfully learned the behavior at home

Three Ds—The variables of complexity (distance, duration, and distractions) that affect a dog's learning process

trainer—The person who is training the dog

treat—A small piece of food used to reinforce a dog during training

treat bag—A wearable bag to hold small pieces of food used to reinforce a dog during training

turn on the marker—The process of pairing the sound of a word or clicker with a piece of food so that the dog learns the sound predicts food

unconditioned stimulus—A stimulus that occurs naturally and causes an automatic response

verbal cue—A word a dog perceives as an indicator to perform a behavior

verbal marker—A word used to mark a dog's behavior that bridges the gap between the time the behavior happens and the delivery of the reinforcer

Reference List

Coppinger, Raymond, and Lorna Coppinger, *Dogs: A New Understanding of Canine Origin, Behavior and Evolution,* Chicago, Illinois, The University of Chicago Press, 2001, 206-211.

Lumen Learning, Basic Principles of Operant Conditioning: Thorndike's Law of Effect, Lumen Boundless Psychology, https://courses.lumenlearning.com/boundless-psychology/chapter/operant-conditioning/, accessed December 19, 2021.

McGreevy, P.D., and R.A Boakes, *Carrots and Sticks: Principles of Animal Training,* Cambridge, New York, Cambridge University Press, 2007, 31.

Merriam-Webster, s.v., "systematic," accessed December 19, 2021, https://www.merriam-webster.com/dictionary/systematic.

Miller, Pat, Peaceable Paws Dog & Puppy Training, https://peaceablepaws.com, accessed December 19, 2021.

Todd, PhD, Zazie, "Positive Reinforcement and Dog Training VII: Summary and Conclusions," *Companion Animal Psychology* (website), August 15, 2012, accessed March 9, 2022, https://www.companionanimalpsychology.com/2012/08/positive-reinforcement-and-dog-training.html

White, Steve, Proactive K9, http://www.proactivek9.com, accessed December 19, 2021.

Recommended Reading List

Brown, Sue, *Juvenile Delinquent Dogs: The Complete Guide to Saving Your Sanity and Successfully Living with Your Adolescent Dog*, The Light of Dog, LLC, 2012.

Coppinger, Raymond, and Lorna Coppinger, *Dogs: A New Understanding of Canine Origin, Behavior and Evolution*, University of Chicago Press, 2001.

Miller, Pat, *The Power of Positive Dog Training*, Wiley Publishing, Inc., 2008.

Rogers, Marge, and Eileen Anderson, *Puppy Socialization: What It Is and How to Do It*, Bright Friends Productions, 2021.

Stilwell, Victoria, *The Ultimate Guide to Raising a Puppy: How to Train and Care for Your New Dog*, Ten Speed Press, 2019.

Stilwell, Victoria, *The Secret Language of Dogs: Unlocking the Canine Mind for a Happier Pet*, Ten Speed Press, 2016.

Watson, Natalie Bridger, *Level Up Your Dog Training: How to Teach Your Dog Anything (some assembly required)*, Underfoot Publishing, 2021.

Index

About the Author

Lisa Lyle Waggoner is a passionate advocate for humane, science-based, force-free dog training. She's a Certified Professional Dog Trainer-Knowledge Assessed, a Pat Miller Certified Trainer-Level 2, a Certified Separation Anxiety Trainer, and a faculty member of the Victoria Stilwell Academy for Dog Training and Behavior.

Lisa is the founder of Cold Nose College, a labor of love that has blossomed into a world-renowned center of education for both dog owners and professional trainers. She is dedicated to helping dogs and their owners form a strong bond and enjoy their lives together. The company provides online dog training around the globe. The trainers have special certification in separation anxiety, as well as credentials related to addressing other behavioral issues.

She lives in western North Carolina in the foothills of the Blue Ridge Mountains and shares her life with her husband and business partner, Brad Waggoner, and their two Australian Shepherd dogs, Cody and Cailie. When not working, you'll find her gardening, playing old-time banjo, and wandering with gratitude throughout their seventeen acres known as Blue Moon Hollow.

Printed in Great Britain
by Amazon

12581313R00133